Coaching Psychology

Coaching Psychology
A Practitioner's Guide

Ho Law

WILEY Blackwell

This edition first published 2013

Wiley-Blackwell is an imprint of John Wiley & Sons, formed by the merger of Wiley's global Scientific, Technical and Medical business with Blackwell Publishing.

Registered Office
John Wiley & Sons, Ltd, The Atrium, Southern Gate, Chichester, West Sussex, PO19 8SQ, UK

Editorial Offices
350 Main Street, Malden, MA 02148-5020, USA
9600 Garsington Road, Oxford, OX4 2DQ, UK
The Atrium, Southern Gate, Chichester, West Sussex, PO19 8SQ, UK

For details of our global editorial offices, for customer services, and for information about how to apply for permission to reuse the copyright material in this book please see our website at www.wiley.com/wiley-blackwell.

Library of Congress Cataloging-in-Publication Data

Law, Ho.
Coaching psychology : a practitioners guide / Ho Law.
pages cm
Includes bibliographical references and index.
ISBN 978-1-119-95467-5 (pbk.)
1. Positive psychology. 2. Counseling–Methodology. I. Title.
BF204.6.L39 2013
158.3–dc23

2013014728

A catalogue record for this book is available from the British Library.

Cover image: Ladder to the sun © Mehmet Salih Guler / Getty Images
Cover design by Richard Boxall Design Associates

Set in 11/13.5pt Galliard by SPi Publisher Services, Pondicherry, India
Printed in Malaysia by Ho Printing (M) Sdn Bhd

1 2013

Contents

About the Author

Dr Ho Law is an international consultant and practitioner psychologist, Health and Care Professions Council (HCPC) Registered Occupational Psychologist, Associate Fellow of the British Psychological Society (BPS), Fellow of the Chartered Management Institute (Chartered Manager), Fellow of the Higher Education Academy, Fellow of the Royal Society of Medicine, and BPS Registered Coaching Psychologist, Chartered Scientist, Chartered Psychologist, Registered Applied Psychology Practice Supervisor. Ho has over 25 years of experience in psychology and management consultancy. He has delivered numerous workshops/conference seminars and carried out consultancy work in the UK and abroad. Ho values diversity in people, respects their cultures and believes in equal opportunities for all. He was one of the first equality advisors to the Assistant Permanent Under Secretary of State in the Home Office, and the Deputy Chair of the BPS Standing Committee for Promotion of Equal Opportunities. Ho is passionate about helping people to develop their talents and achieve their full potential through coaching and mentoring. He is a founding member and Chair (2010) of the BPS Special Group in Coaching Psychology; founding director and treasurer of the International Society for Coaching Psychology. Ho has published over 40 papers and received numerous outstanding achievement awards including the Local Promoters for Cultural Diversity Project in 2003, the Positive Image (Business Category) in 2004, and Management Essentials Participating Company in 2005, and is the winner of the first Student-Led Teaching Award (2013) – Best Supervisor. He is the Head of Profession in Coaching Psychology. He is the founder Director of Empsy® Ltd and the President of Empsy® Network for coaching (www.empsy.com). At the University of East London School of Psychology, Ho is a Senior Lecturer, Co-Programme Leader in the MSc Coaching Psychology Programme, Admissions Tutor, and Leader Tutor in the Distance Learning Programme:

http://www.uel.ac.uk/programmes/psychology/postgraduate/coaching psychology-dl.htm

Ho is currently supervising two part-time students' PhDs in education at the University of East London; the students are currently working in the United Arab Emirates.

Foreword

Why has coaching psychology, as a science and a practice, emerged globally in the last few years in so many countries? This is a big question, and this book by Ho Law is part of the evolving narrative and answer to that question. In terms of our performance, be it in life or work, we are, in my view, fundamentally challenged at three levels:

- problem solving
- task/project management and delivery
- people management (both self and other).

Most educational systems address very well the first two of these areas in terms of transmissional learning, skills and knowledge. However, there is a gap apparent in how we manage ourselves and others, which might explain this emergence of coaching and, more recently, coaching psychology as an applied behavioural science in both life and work domains.

This practice we call coaching is about a conversation and the skills of that conversation. Scott (2002) suggests 'that our work, our relationships and in fact our very lives succeed or fail gradually, then suddenly, one conversation at a time'. Whitmore (2002) points to the inherent challenges and opportunity of this coaching conversation in terms of 'unlocking our potential to maximise our performance'. However, coaching psychology as a continually and fast-emerging domain in its own right, is about the evidence-based understanding, not only of this practice and process we call coaching but also about understanding and explaining the interference (Gallwey, 2001), both internal and external, that we humans experience in terms of mastering this conversation with both ourselves and others. Out of this conversation emerge the values and the goals and the actions which are likely to build on strengths, create a compelling vision for the future and cement relationships.

This conversation is about how best we can harness our individual and collective potential, and perform in the challenging, uncertain, complex and volatile world that faces us in our life and work every day. Stephen Palmer quite rightly suggested in a recent discussion that, 'You can take the coaching out of psychology but you cannot take the psychology out of coaching'. Coaching psychology and how the mind works goes to the very heart of how we manage and lead both ourselves and others.

Ho Law has been a key figure in the emergence of coaching psychology in the UK. In 2005 at a conference organized by the British Psychological Societies, Special Group in Coaching Psychology I was fortunate to begin a conversation with Ho and others, which informed the setting up of the Coaching Psychology Group (CPG) within the Division of Work and Organisational Psychology (DWOP) within the Psychological Society of Ireland (PSI). More recently this conversation led to the setting up of a Higher Diploma Programme in Coaching/Coaching Psychology in 2010 and subject to final confirmation, the first Master's programme in Coaching Psychology for graduate psychologists in Ireland. This programme will run from September 2013 in tandem with a similar Master's programme for non-psychologists. Coaching science and practice will, for the first time, come together in Ireland in the School of Applied Psychology, University College Cork. This will be only one of three such programmes in the UK and Ireland.

While the literature around coaching, generally, is extensive, such literature in the coaching psychology space is not as extensive, but is expanding. The ubiquitous beliefs-based approach to coaching is still all too evident and the challenge remains to build on and expand the current evidence base and to professionalize the practice of coaching and coaching psychology.

That is why the contribution of Ho Law and his new practical guide is particularly important and timely. Linking theory to practice and building on his previous publication, *The Psychology of Coaching, Mentoring and Learning* (Law, Ireland and Hussain, 2007; Law, 2014), this companion workbook is the first to provide practical, step-by-step guidance and exercises for the trainee coaching psychologist. It is also an invaluable resource for anyone, including experienced coaching practitioners interested in coaching or CPD and in particular the evidence-based approach of coaching psychology. In this welcome publication, Ho is most certainly applying the theory and putting the evidence base of psychology and adult/child learning into coaching.

Coaching is a language that leaders, managers, educators, health professionals, soldiers and indeed anyone that chooses in awareness to take responsibility for themselves and others, must learn. Coaching psychology is an area of study, research and practice that can add to this language. Coaching psychology is now part of a global narrative. This book is one which adds to our understanding of coaching psychology in practice and one which I will recommend as a core text to my students as they explore coaching and coaching psychology as an effective process for change, growth, improved performance and well-being in life and work.

Hugh O'Donovan
Programme Co-Director, Higher Diploma
Coaching/Coaching Psychology
University College Cork

References

Gallwey, W.T. (2000) *The Inner Game of Work: Focus*, Random House, New York.

Law, H.C. (2014) *The Psychology of Coaching, Mentoring and Learning*, 2nd edn, John Wiley & Sons, Ltd, Chichester.

Law, H.C., Ireland, S. and Hussain, Z. (2007) *The Psychology of Coaching, Mentoring and Learning*, John Wiley & Sons, Ltd, Chichester.

Palmer, S. and Whybrow, A. (eds) (2007) *Handbook of Coaching Psychology: A Guide for Practitioners*, Routledge, London.

Scott, S. (2002) *Fierce Conversations: Achieving Success in Work and in Life, One Conversation at a Time*, London, Piatkus.

Whitmore, J. (2002) *Coaching for Performance: Growing People, Performance and Purpose*, Nicholas Brealey, London.

Preface

Coaching is a growing industry and is continuously expanding to new fields. There is a strong interest in coaching practice especially in the context of the current global challenges we face in business, economics, education, finance and human resources. Leadership and coaching leaders in their professional development is increasingly important.

Coaching psychology is emerging as a new discipline. The British Psychological Society's (BPS) Special Group in Coaching Psychology (SGCP) was formed in 2004; and a Register of Coaching Psychologists was set up in 2012 to indicate those practitioner psychologists who have specialist expertise in coaching psychology. In 2008, the Society for Coaching Psychology was founded and in 2011, it was re-named to the International Society for Coaching Psychology.

As interest in coaching psychology continues to grow globally, there is an increasing need to train coaches, psychologists and allied professions to develop coaching psychology as a profession. Coaching psychology as a subject of studies and research is being offered by universities such as the University of East London, University College Cork, the City University London, the University of Sydney and the Federal University of Rio de Janeiro, to name a few.

My motivation to write this book is to satisfy the need of providing a book which can serve both seasoned practitioners in coaching or psychology and students or trainees who are studying coaching psychology as part of their learning and professional development. While there are many publications on coaching, there are not many on coaching psychology. What makes the book *The Psychology of Coaching, Mentoring and Learning* (Law, Ireland and Hussain, 2007; Law, 2014) special is that it grounds the model of coaching on learning theories, and offers a dual perspective of coaching and mentoring. This book is designed to follow the same structure and coaching philosophy as *The Psychology of Coaching, Mentoring and*

Learning, and offers the reader a wider range of coaching techniques and more in-depth treatment in practical exercises, with a specific focus on helping readers to translate the understanding of theories into their professional practice. For instance, this *Practitioner's Guide* offers additional tools and exercises on gestalt approaches, mindfulness exercises and reflective practice within the coaching context.

While I would strongly recommend you to read *The Psychology of Coaching, Mentoring and Learning* as a companion to this *Guide*, this book is also designed to stand alone for use as a practical guide or workbook to help you to learn and develop as a coaching psychologist. However, I cannot claim that this is a definitive book on coaching psychology for practitioners. As a single authored book, there are bound to be areas of coaching and coaching psychology that it has not covered. The views, philosophy, models of coaching, psychological theories, tools and techniques offered here merely represent some of the knowledge and experience that I have acquired over the course of my own learning and professional development – 30 years in my professional engagements in psychology, and more specifically 10 years in coaching psychology.

Coaching is about learning … I continue to learn in my coaching, teaching, supervision and research; and it is a pleasure to share some of the joy and excitement in learning along the way with my coachees, students and colleagues, which in turn facilitates further learning. Writing this book represents the sharing of those loved experiences and moments of learning and development. I hope you enjoy reading this *Practitioner's Guide* and actively engage in the learning and practice of some of the exercises that are relevant to your work, professional or personal development. I welcome sharing the experience of your learning and practice; feedback and comments are most welcome. Please write to:

Ho Law PhD CPsychol CSci CMgr MISCP(Accred)
AFBPsS FCMI FHEA
PO Box 696
Peterborough PE2 9YQ
England, UK

Email:
Personal: ho.law@ntlworld.com
Company: ho.law@empsy.com
http://www.empsy.com/
Twitter: @empsy
www.twitter.com/empsy
University: law2@uel.ac.uk
http://www.uel.ac.uk/psychology/staff/hochunglaw/
Internet: drholaw@gmail.com

Acknowledgements

This book was written in parallel with the writing of *The Psychology of Coaching, Mentoring and Learning* over an 18-month period. The 'writing journey' was punctuated with the loss of my father who passed away in Hong Kong on 9 May in 2012, aged 96. I had to travel to Hong Kong to attend his funeral at short notice. I was deeply moved by all the support that I received from my colleagues at the University of East London, who stepped in to do the student supervision, marking and double-marking of the assignments within a very tight schedule; their support has made me feel part of the team and community within which I feel blessed. There is a Chinese proverb which says that it is easy to add icing on the cake, it is difficult to give support to someone in destitution. It is the time of hardship that tests true colleagueship and friendship. I thank them for being such great teams.

My father's middle and first names are Kai Sin which means 'showing' 'kindness'. It resonates with the spirit of coaching and mentoring. I shall hold onto this spirit dearly in my heart and attempt to manifest this unconditional kindness in everything that I do. And within this spirit, I would like to express my gratitude to those who have shown their kindness and helped me along the way when I truly needed them, not only in writing this book but also my life journey.

As in the acknowledgements in *The Psychology of Coaching, Mentoring and Learning*, I shall reiterate here:

There are inevitably many names to acknowledge, including those of family and friends, who have been taken for granted during this period, and many unintentional omissions. So without mentioning every possible individual, I shall list (in alphabetical order) some of those who have continued to inspire me as well as some of the contributors, the unsung heroes and organizations within the context of my journey in coaching.

Thanks go to:

- Dr Carla Gibbes – Senior Lecturer at the University of East London for her kindness and support.
- Liz Hall – for communicating the concept of narrative coaching to wider professional communities via *Coaching at Work*.
- Trevor Hall, OBE, CBE – who has continued to inspire me in championing equality and diversity in my cross-cultural journey, in my career, and life.
- Professor Stephen Palmer – for his continuous support and updating the Foreword.
- Kaemorine Prendergast – for her kindness and righteousness in championing equality.
- Aquilina Reginald – my former coaching student for helping me to introduce coaching to nursing and contributing to the case study on leadership coaching within the healthcare sector in Malta.
- Dr Donald Ridley – Principal Lecturer at the University of East London, for his support and guidance.
- Christine Stocker-Gibson – for contributing to some of the case studies.
- Michael White, Dulwich Centre – who inspired and trained me in narrative approaches from down under. His spirit will continue to manifest in my narrative coaching.

Organizations that have provided me with support and information for this edition include:

- Association for Coaching.
- British Psychological Society's (BPS) Special Group in Coaching Psychology.
- Chartered Management Institute (CMI).
- European Mentoring and Coaching Council (EMCC).
- International Coach Federation (ICF) for giving permission to publish the results of its Global Coaching Study.
- International Society for Coaching Psychology.

Most of all, I would like to thank all those who I have come across in my coaching/mentoring journey, in many spaces and places, from the place where I live, people of Peterborough, and the neighbouring areas within Cambridgeshire. It was from this place that a number of coaching and mentoring programmes took place, for communities, for individuals, for private and public organizations. It was from this place that some of the case studies have been consolidated. It was from this place that the Universal Integrated Framework was developed through our lived experience.

And from the place where I work, in particular, I would like to thank all my colleagues in the School of Psychology, University of East London where the 2012 London Olympics and Paralympics took place. The place truly embodies the spirit of the games – that is, to inspire individuals to achieve their highest potential – this is the spirit of coaching and mentoring too!

There are many more of you out there who have contributed to my understanding. To you, perhaps the unacknowledged, I offer my thanks too.

Ho Law
Peterborough, England, UK

Disclaimers

The views expressed in this book are those of the author, and not those of the publisher, or Empsy Ltd, or UEL, or anyone else. This is in no way affected by the right reserved by the author to edit the cases published. Owing to the requirement for confidentiality within our code of ethics, the context/stories of some case studies may have been adapted and individual identities kept anonymous. If the case studies documented in this book have omitted any partners' contribution, this is entirely unintentional.

1

Introduction

Hello! A very warm welcome to the introduction of this book – *Coaching Psychology: A Practitioner's Guide*. I assume that you are reading this book because you have either trained in coaching psychology (or related disciplines such as coaching, mentoring, counselling and psychology), or are a seasoned practitioner. The purpose of this book is to provide a guide for practitioners within the field of coaching psychology and its allied professions in coaching and mentoring. Or perhaps you are simply interested in the subject; that is OK too; and I welcome you to this 'journey' of coaching psychology in practice. While based on the key text *The Psychology of Coaching, Mentoring and Learning*, this is a book in its own right and does not assume any prior knowledge. Accordingly, while *The Psychology of Coaching, Mentoring and Learning* is recommended as a valuable companion read, you will find that this book stands alone for use as a practical guide or workbook for your practice and/or continuous self-/professional development. In some ways this book can be seen as the 'inverse' of *The Psychology of Coaching, Mentoring and Learning*, in that the latter offers a detailed account of theory with an overview of practice, while the former offers an overview of theory with a more detailed account of practice. It is anticipated that many practitioners will want to read both books.

Coaching Psychology: A Practitioner's Guide, First Edition. Ho Law.

Historically, coaching psychology was applied in the domains of sports and exercise. Recent debate on coaching psychology seems to be around the following areas (Cavanagh and Lane, 2012a,b):

- coaching models
- professionalism
- evidence-based practice.

This book will address each of the above areas.

Aims

While this book follows the same overall structure as *The Psychology of Coaching, Mentoring and Learning*, its emphasis has shifted firmly to coaching practice. It aims to show you how theories and principles of psychology can be applied in coaching, mentoring and learning for individuals and organizations, and also offers extended examples and practical, step-by-step exercises for you to complete.

Who is it For?

This book is written for the following groups:

- Readers of *The Psychology of Coaching, Mentoring and Learning* who would like a more practical guide, dedicated to implementation of the ideas.
- Coaches, mentors, trainers and other professionals who may not be psychologists and do not want detailed theoretical material, but require a guide for practice along with a grounding in the psychological theory that underpins the techniques and approaches.
- Psychologists who want to apply their experience to coaching, mentoring and training.

Whoever you are – coaches or psychologists – I hope you will find this book an invaluable resource for your continuous professional development and as a reference for your coaching practice.

Content in a Nutshell

Chapter 1 aims to guide readers to gain a rapid understanding about the nature of the book and to find the information easily. It provides a rationale for writing this book with an overall structure and brief description of each chapter. It also provides suggestions of how to use the book for different levels of readers according to their interest, experience and professional competence. Chapter 2 provides a brief outline of the developments of the coaching and coaching psychology professions. It then describes the practical steps of coaching psychology in practice with emphases on awareness of ethical and practical issues.

Chapter 3 provides an overview of the core principles of positive psychology and learning theories. The definitions of coaching psychology and its related concepts: coaching, mentoring and learning, are discussed in Chapter 4. Chapter 5 describes how you may introduce a coaching programme into an organization. Chapter 6 first describes the differences between models and techniques, with two examples – GROW and Universal Integrative Framework (UIF); it then provides guidance on how to build your own model and apply it in practice. The techniques and their related practical exercises that fit within the structure of the UIF and the revised Integrative Learning System (ILS) are described in Chapter 7 and Chapter 8, respectively. Chapter 9 provides a number of case studies and invites you to collect your own. Chapter 10 describes how you can take steps to evaluate your coaching practice within the evidence-based framework. Finally, Chapter 11 provides a personal reflection and further tips and resources for coaching psychology practice.

How to Use this Book

Depending on who you are, and your level of experience in coaching psychology, you can use this book in many different ways. For the first reading, you may like to skim through and then return to those elements that you are particularly interested in at a later time. Whoever you are, I recommend Chapter 2 on ethics as a 'must-read' before anyone practises coaching with other people. Once you have understood the ethical principles and relevant theories or concepts, you can pick and choose your exercises to suit your need.

Exercise boxes focus on linking theory to practices. Unlike many other coaching or psychology books, this book contains many exercises to help you to apply your learning into practice. These coaching exercises are relevant to the topic of each chapter.

For those who just want a few 'how to do' tips using coaching psychology, you may simply look at the techniques that you want to learn and practise the 'guided' exercises in Chapters 7 and 8, respectively.

If you are a coaching trainer or tutor and wish to use this book as a training guide, you can first read the whole book to make sure that you understand all the essential elements, and know where to find things as a reference. Divide your training programme into three parts (beginning – middle – end). Chapters 2–4 can be used as an introduction to your training course. This is an important and yet quite a non-trivial task. You need to succinctly describe the history, epistemology and definition of coaching psychology without going through the details and ask your participants/students to read the chapters afterward as references; explain ethics (using the 6Rs principles in Chapter 2) at an early stage of the training programme and certainly before any exercises are commenced.

If you are a novice, you may like to read this book from start to finish, following its logical progression. Don't attempt to read the whole book in one go. Some of the chapters are quite 'heavy' and even a trained psychology practitioner would find it thought provoking and demanding. Try to devise a reading plan that fits into your personal development, for example, preparing for an examination, or doing a training course, say, over a three-month period.

When reading this book, you may find it useful to make notes along the way of techniques to use in your own life and work. Keep practising and keep a reflective log (a template is included in the Appendix to this book).

2

Current State of Coaching and Coaching Psychology

Where are you now?

Introduction

This chapter provides a summary of the developments in coaching and mentoring. You are encouraged to assess yourself in terms of your own coaching practice; identify your strengths and opportunities. In doing so, you will be able to position your practice within the coaching market. By the end of working through this chapter, together with the supplementary reading and practice, you should be able to:

- Gain an understanding of coaching and the coaching psychology profession, its development and why it is a growing industry.
- Describe the key aspects of the coach–coachee relationship in relation to the role of the coach and code of ethics.
- Describe the six ethical principles in relation to the code of ethics.

Developments in Coaching and Coaching Psychology

The coaching industry

The coaching industry has grown exponentially in recent years. The total turnover of coaching is estimated to be more than $2 billion globally (ICF & PricewaterhouseCoopers, 2012). It is predicted to continue to grow in spite of

Coaching Psychology: A Practitioner's Guide, First Edition. Ho Law.

the current economic climate. Each month, you may come across articles about coaching in papers and magazines and how it can be used to leverage individual and organizational performance.

Exercise 2.1

Pause for a moment...

1. Make a list of the cases that you have recently read about applications of coaching (this may come from books, newspapers, journals and/or magazines):

   ____
   ____
   ____
   ____

2. Select one case listed above, think about:
   a. What differences has coaching intervention made?
   b. How did coaching make the differences?

   ____
   ____
   ____
   ____

3. Reflect on your work, how would you make a positive difference to others and your organization, community or society?

   ____
   ____
   ____
   ____

The Coaching Matrix

While there are diverse services, the coaching industry can be divided into four types:

1. Academic and professional institutions
2. Business and management consultancies

3. Independent practitioners
4. Internal coaches and mentors.

Academic and professional institutions

Academic and professional institutions include colleges of further education, higher education, universities and professional bodies such as the British Psychological Society (BPS), Institute of Directors (IoD), the Chartered Institute of Management (CIM) and the Chartered Institute of Personnel and Development (CIPD). These organizations unusually have in-house coaching or mentoring programmes. Some of them also offer external training programmes and courses on coaching and coaching psychology, ranging from tailor-made short vocational courses to formal academic qualifications (certificates, diplomas, masters or doctorates).

There are a number of professional organizations in coaching and coaching psychology; these include:

- Association for Coaching (AC)
- Association of Integrative Coach-Therapist Professionals (AICTP)
- Association for Professional Executive Coaching and Supervision (APECS)
- BACP Coaching – a division of the British Association for Counselling and Psychotherapy
- BPS Special Group in Coaching Psychology (SGCP)
- Chartered Management Institute (CMI) Coaching Division
- European Mentoring and Coaching Council (EMCC)
- International Coach Federation (ICF)
- International Society for Coaching Psychology (ISCP).

The above list is not exhaustive, you may like to add more. Which professional organization do you belong to?

Business and management consultancies

Coaching is a market-led discipline; many consultancies offer coaching as part of their services. The typical aims of coaching include improving:

- career development
- conflict resolution
- performance
- profit

- return on investment (ROI)
- human capital
- relationships
- work/life balance.

Independent practitioners

These may be individual sole traders or large companies. There are a large number of independent practitioners in coaching (according to the ICF 2012 survey, it is estimated that there are around 47,500 professional coaches around the globe). Their backgrounds are diverse, ranging from education, training, personnel, business and management consultancy, human resources to marketing. From my personal observation, many individuals who claim to be a life coach tend to be sole traders who may or may not have another job to supplement their income.

Exercise 2.2

Pause for a moment … Think about:

1. What challenges do you think independent practitioners might face?

____

____

____

____

2. What are the issues or concerns that you might have?

____

____

____

____

Although many sole traders often have a low profile, they do provide quite a competitive market as their costs and fees are relatively lower than organizations. The presence of such large numbers of individual private coaches in an unregulated industry does pose concerns in terms of ethics and standards.

Internal coaches and mentors

Internal coaches provide coaching services within their organization. Very often, this may be in addition to their current job title, roles and responsibilities. For example, a lot of colleges and universities offer coaching support for their students as well as staff. Some organizations (large or small) offer their employees on-job coaching and mentoring as part of their development and training.

Exercise 2.3

Pause for a moment … Think about:

What are the advantages and disadvantages of being an internal coach within an organization?

____

____

____

____

Internal coaches are also competing in the coaching market. They have distinct advantages as they understand the organizational context much better than the external consultant. Also their professional rates tend to be much lower than those of the external consultants (part of their salary); many organizations prefer to develop their own coaches for their in-house coaching programme.

The four types of coaching providers can be summarized as shown in Table 2.1.

Table 2.1 Coaching matrix in practice

	Internal	*External*
Corporate	Internal coaches and mentors (e.g. Academic and professional institutions)	Consultants (e.g. Business and management)
Private	Personal coach and mentor (Private arrangements)	Independent practitioners

Exercise 2.4

Pause for a moment ... Referring to Table 2.1, reflect on your own position:

If you are already a coach, which category of coach do you belong to?

What are the challenges, pros and cons of this position?

____

____

____

____

Whether you are already a coach or not, as what type of coach would you like to position yourself in the future, and why?

____

____

____

____

What are the expected challenges, advantages and disadvantages that you would envisage in such a position?

____

____

____

____

Developing Your Skills and Knowledge

Exercise 2.5

What skills do you think are critical for a new coach to develop?

____

____

____

____

You may be interested to compare your answers to the above exercise with McKenna and Davis's (2009) four 'active ingredients' of the variance in successful outcomes of coaching:

1. client factors (40%)
2. the relationship or alliance (30%)
3. placebo or hope (15%)
4. theory and technique (15%).

The above list suggests that knowing the theory and techniques only contributes to a small part of the coaching success. A successful outcome is largely due to the coachee's own effort and the skill of the coach to develop and maintain a good coaching relationship with the coachee. By reading this book, you will further develop your knowledge and skills in coaching psychology and learn how they can be integrated in your own practice. However, before you get going, it is important for you to understand about ethical principles for coaching and coaching psychology. Practising ethically will help you to develop and maintain a good (safe and professional) coaching relationship.

Ethical Principles

First things first – do it ethically

Most coaches, and managers who buy in their services as interventions, would agree that the code of ethics is important for their practice. To be a professional coach/mentor requires you to observe professional ethics. Many professional bodies have their own codes of ethics and conduct and require their members to observe them accordingly. Some business schools provide training in ethics. Coaches/mentors may be sued for unethical behaviour. A number of professional organizations require their members to have a professional indemnity insurance policy. Legislation such as the Equality Act or Companies Act embodies ethical principles and corporate social responsibility.

Many people believe that ethics simply involves learning what is right or wrong, and then doing the right thing. For instance no one would debate about the minimum standard that one should 'do no harm to clients'. However, in numerous coaching and mentoring situations the application of ethical principles may not be so clear.

This section focuses on the practical implication of ethics in coaching and mentoring. I shall first define what ethics are about. A generic set of ethical guidance that is based on the knowledge of many coaching and mentoring professional organizations will be described.

Definition of ethics

Exercise 2.6

How do you define ethics?

What are they for?

____

____

____

____

The term 'ethics' (or *ethik* in Middle English or *ethique* in Old French) originates from the Greek word *ēthikos* (ethical) as in *ēthos.* A quick search on the internet provides the following definitions:

- 'The study of the general nature of morals and of the specific moral choices to be made by a person; moral philosophy' (The Free Dictionary, 2008).
- 'The rules or standards governing the conduct of a person or the members of a profession' (The Free Dictionary, 2008), such as medical ethics or in this context, coaching ethics.
- 'The principles of right and wrong that are accepted by an individual or a social group' (Wordnet, 2008).

Adopting Rowson's (2001) and Law's (2006a) definitions, ethical principles can be defined as the rules which coaches and mentors are committed to in their practice. These rules embody your values as coaches and mentors that justify your moral judgements and actions. This definition represents 'a sequence of cognitive processes' (Law, 2006a) as follows (see Figure 2.1):

1. morality
2. values
3. commitment
4. rules
5. rationale
6. professional judgement.

Also see Duffy and Passmore (2010) who further explored the above cognitive process using grounded theory (semi-structured interviews and focused group study of six experienced coaching psychologists); and devel-

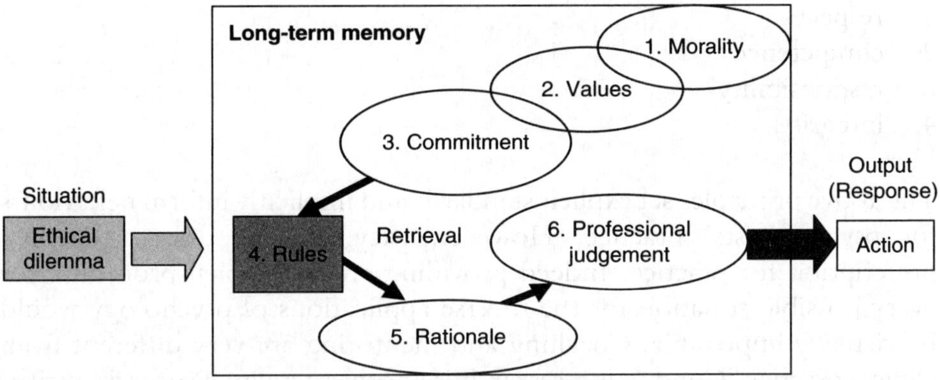

Figure 2.1 Ethical principles as 'a sequence of cognitive processes'

oped an ethical decision-making framework. This involves awareness, reflection and exploration of different options. Engaging stakeholders and supervision are part of the decision-making process.

The aim of ethical principles is to protect coachees/mentees and the public from dangerous coaching practice. The objectives are to:

- ensure safety
- benefit clients
- protect clients
- manage boundaries
- manage conflict.

Codes of ethics and standards of practice are usually included in professional organizations as mentioned earlier.

The code of ethics for coaching or coaching psychology is a form of self-regulation; members of a professional organization are required to abide by their own code only. The exception is the British Psychological Society. Its members are not only expected to observe the BPS's Code of Ethics and Conduct, for those who practise psychology (which usually means Chartered Psychologists), but they are also required to be registered with the Health and Care Professions Council (HCPC) and observe its Standards of Conduct, Performance and Ethics. This is due to a change in recent legislation in the UK. At the time of writing, the question, 'Will the HCPC registration apply to coaches and mentors?' is a topic for debate. The BPS SGCP is working towards providing a register for coaches and coaching psychologists.

The BPS Code of Ethics and Conduct provides four general overarching principles for psychologists. These are based on the following four Principles of Ethics:

1. respect
2. competence
3. responsibility
4. integrity.

The above principles set explicit standards and implicitly inform behaviours for psychologists' practice. However, they do not offer a detailed prescription for practice. Indeed providing an operational procedure for every possible situation for the diverse applications of psychology would be virtually impossible. Coaching and mentoring are very different from clinical practice. Conducting research is another activity. Research institutions such as universities have their own code of ethics for researchers and students to follow.

The Guidelines for Professional Practice in Counselling Psychology provide some practical guidance that may be relevant to coaching and mentoring. They expand the principle of responsibility in terms of the responsibility to:

1. self and clients
2. self and colleagues
3. self and society.

Linking the standard of practice to ethical codes and drawing from a number of coaching organizations, Law (2010) proposed six ethical principles called the 6Rs of Ethical Principles for the Code of Ethics and Practice for the Society for Coaching Psychology. These are:

1. rights
2. respect
3. recognition
4. relationship
5. representation
6. responsibility.

The principles of rights and respect are interwoven in practice; they are usually expressed together as one. The above ethical principles define our code of practice as follows:

- Rights and respect – Respect the rights of coachees as human beings. Coaches should obtain informed consent from the coachees about using their information for various purposes. They should maintain confidentiality of their coachees and be open to respond to their requests for information. All these arrangements should be discussed with the coachees and they should be provided with an explicit coaching contract at the first session. Also, coaches need be sensitive to coachees' individual and cultural differences in terms of their age, gender, disability, race, religion/belief, sexual orientation and so on.

- Recognition – Recognize the standards and limits of one's own competence. Coaches need to be aware of their competency in coaching and recognize their own limit. They should practise within the boundary of their competence.
- Relationship – Establish good relationships and trust with coachees. Coaches need to establish a rapport with the coachee and maintain a good coaching relationship throughout their interaction. A coaching/mentoring relationship is 'unique' in comparison with other professions, and is a so-called 'double triad relationship' (Law, 2006a). This is because coaching, especially executive coaching, involves different stakeholders – coaches, coachees and customers. Coaches need to take particular care about any possible dual/multiple relationships; and when these occur, clarify the multiple roles and resolve any conflicts that they might cause.
- Representation – Represent oneself and profession accurately and honestly. Coaches and mentors should represent themselves and professions appropriately. They should not act in a manner that might bring their professional organization into disrepute.
- Responsibility – Take professional responsibility for oneself, one's coachees/mentees, the stakeholders and the society. Coaches and mentors need to have professional indemnity insurance to protect themselves and coachees/mentees against liability. They should encourage coachees/mentees to take their own responsibility for the coaching or mentoring outcome. However, coaches and mentors are responsible for evaluating the coaching outcomes in terms of their effectiveness and efficiency and keeping appropriate coaching records. Coaches and mentors should also take responsibility for any coachee's unethical behaviour. In addition, coaches and mentors should continue to learn and develop as part of their continuous professional development (CPD) and supervision.

Ethical coaching is a reflective practice where the coaches ask themselves, coachees and all the other stakeholders a set of ethical questions. From the literature review (see Law, 2003, 2009), I have compiled a set of questions that are relevant to coaching in Exercise 2.7.

Exercise 2.7

How ethical is your behaviour?

How ethical is your organization as a whole?

How vulnerable are you within this complex relationship?

What are the core values that define your organization?

What are the core values that define you as a person?

Who are the customers, coachees and/or mentees?

Whose benefit has priority?

Whose interests is the coaching psychologist serving?

What is the coach's ethical duty?

What is the responsibility of the coaching psychologist to manage different values and interests between all the stakeholders?

How are the differences managed?

Is there potential for abuse of power?

What are the issues of confidentiality?

What are the implications of vicarious liability?

Have you defined the problem accurately?

How would you define the problem if you stood on the other side of the fence?

How did this situation occur in the first place?

To whom and to what do you give your loyalty as a coach, coachee and as a client of the organization?

What is your intention in making this decision?

How does this intention compare with the probable results?

Whom could your decision or action injure?

Can you discuss the problem with the affected parties before you make your decision?

Are you confident that your position will be as valid over a long period of time as it seems now?

Could you disclose without qualm your decision or action to your supervisor, your colleagues, the clients, your family, society as a whole?

What is the symbolic potential of your action if understood or misunderstood?

Under what conditions would you allow exceptions to your standards?

Chapter Summary

This chapter has provided you with an overview of the developments in coaching and coaching psychology. In defining the key skills in preparation for developing a coach–coachee relationship, this chapter has argued a strong case for taking a more proactive role in considering issues of ethics and their practice. I have introduced a set of ethical principles (6Rs) and recommend coaches and mentors to apply them in their practice. To summarize, it is worth reminding readers of the following ethical considerations (Law, 2005a, b and c, 2006a):

- Do no harm.
- Apply ethical principles effectively in everything we do.
- Aim to serve coachees well.
- Act in the best interest of the clients and their organizations.
- Respect differences.
- Observe confidentiality.
- Recognize one's role.
- Be informed about legal and employment requirements that override limits on confidentiality for the particular context.
- Discuss with coachees if breaking confidentiality is necessary.
- Make these limits clear to coachees.
- Where there is a specific duty or legal requirement for disclosure to a third party, warn the coachee during the sessions that if they tell you more, you will be under an obligation to act.
- Supplement verbal description of limits with a written contract.
- Share information on a 'need to know' basis (when practising with extended confidentiality).
- Be trustworthy.
- Trust coachees' choices and control in terms of both their unconscious and consciousness.
- Seek informed consent explicitly in advance.
- Help coachees to make informed choices and take their own responsibility.
- Prepare to work through conflicting stakeholder value perspectives.
- Understand that helping coachees to act is much better than the coach having to act.
- Understand that every interaction has its ethical implications.
- Continue professional development and supervision.
- Discuss the coaching dilemma with your supervisor, coaching colleagues and/or manager.

3

The Foundation of Coaching Psychology

Being positive and learning how to learn

Introduction

Positive psychology and theories of learning are regarded as the two pillars that form the foundation of coaching psychology. This chapter will briefly highlight these theories and explain why and how they are applicable to coaching. It describes the learning theories in psychology that are applicable to coaching; and attempts to link learning to coaching. This will include Kolb's (1984) experiential learning cycle, and how the learning cycle can be mapped onto the coaching process and its implications for reflective practice as part of continuous professional development. You will be shown how to carry out your own reflective learning with a step-by-step procedure (template included in the Appendix).

In this chapter, I shall first describe positive psychology in relation to coaching and then give an overall review of literature on the psychology of learning. This includes:

- the learning process
- reflective learning
- constructive-developmental theories
- social learning theories.

Coaching Psychology: A Practitioner's Guide, First Edition. Ho Law.

By the end of reading this chapter (completing all the exercises) you should be able to:

1. Explain the foundation of coaching psychology.
2. Explain how positive psychology and learning theories may be used in coaching.
3. Use positive psychology and learning in your reflection and coaching practice.

How About Being Positive? Positive Psychology and its Implication for Coaching

- How happy are you?
- What enables happiness?
- What are the effects of autonomy and self-regulation on motivation?
- How do optimism and hope affect health?
- What constitutes wisdom?
- How do talent and creativity come to fruition?
- How positive are you?

In recent years, there has been an increasing interest in pursuing the above questions. Seligman and Csikszentmihalyi (2000) have effectively explored the answers and introduced a new discipline called positive psychology. Positive psychology focuses on the positive aspects of human characteristics and behaviours (such as positive emotions, strength-based characters and healthy institutions) rather than the negative aspects, on which Martin Seligman argues that clinical psychologists and psychotherapists tend to focus (Peterson and Seligman, 2004). One would expect that positive psychology is hugely relevant to coaching as it shares a similar point of departure from counselling or psychotherapy and focuses on the peak performance of individuals. It resonates with the concept of flow – a state when people experience a sense of joy as they are performing at their peak (Csikszentmihalyi, 1991). Both positive psychology and coaching psychology are concerned with the improvement of performance and well-being (Linley and Harrington, 2005). Thus positive psychology provides us with a foundation to coaching practice (Law, 2014). Despite its modern appearance, positive psychology can be traced back throughout European psychology (see Allport, 1961; Jahoda, 1958; James, 1902; Jung, 1933; Linley and Joseph, 2004a; Maslow, 1968; Roger, 1963).

In relation to a positive fulfilling life, positive psychology focuses on:

1. Positive emotions – the pleasant life.
2. Positive characters – the engaged life.
3. Positive institutions – the meaningful life.

Positive emotions consist of three domains along the temporal dimension:

1. The past – the positive experience from the past gives us a sense of satisfaction, contentment, fulfilment, pride and serenity.
2. The present – we can positively engage in the present moment and thereby experience joy, ecstasy, calm, zest, ebullience, pleasure and possibly 'flow'.
3. The future – we can look towards the future positively with a sense of optimism, hope, faith and trust.

Positive psychology is clearly relevant to coaching in terms of its enquiry into human experiences such as happiness, wisdom, creativity and strengths. The latter provides a significant potential for human development and therefore should benefit coaching, for example, using the individual's signature character strengths (strength-based coaching). As said, counselling and psychotherapy tend to focus on what is wrong with their clients – especially their psychological problems. In contrast, strength-based coaching (SBC) focuses on what the coachees are good at and their signature strengths within themselves. This is not to deny that there are no problems in life. However, having acknowledged that there are challenges out there and that life consists of struggles, the emphasis is that there is much more to life than problems. SBC reminds coachees about their signature character strengths and resources so that they can shift their focus from the problem to the solution and achieve a positive outcome. I shall briefly outline these signature character strengths next.

Peterson and Seligman (2004) have identified 24 'signature character strengths' (SCS). These are clustered into six dimensions and summarized in Table 3.1.

You may have already been using your signature character strengths. However, consciously applying your character strengths will improve performance, leverage your life/work and help you to achieve greater happiness. I shall show you how to first identify your signature character strengths and then how you may apply them in your own life and/or coaching situation.

Table 3.1 Summary of SCS

Cluster	*SCS dimensions*	*SCS elements*	*Description*
1	Wisdom and knowledge	1. Creativity – originality, ingenuity 2. Curiosity – interest, novelty seeking, openness to experience 3. Open mindedness – evidence-based judgement, critical thinking 4. Love of learning 5. Perspective – wisdom	Cognitive strengths that consist of knowledge acquisition and its application
2	Courage	6. Bravery – valour 7. Persistence 8. Integrity – authenticity, honesty 9. Vitality – zest, enthusiasm, vigour, energy	Emotional strengths that involve the exercise of will to accomplish goals in the face of challenges, dangers, difficulties, fears, obstacles, pains or threats
3	Humanity	10. Love 11. Kindness – generosity, nurture, care, compassion, altruistic love, niceness 12. Social intelligence – emotional intelligence, personal intelligence	Interpersonal strengths that involve 'tending' and 'befriending' others
4	Justice	13. Citizenship – social responsibility, loyalty, teamwork 14. Fairness 15. Leadership	Civic strengths that underlie healthy community life
5	Temperance	16. Forgiveness and mercy 17. Humility and modesty 18. Prudence 19. Self-regulation – self-control	Strengths that protect against excess
6	Transcendence	20. Appreciation of beauty and excellence – awe, wonder, elevation, transcendence 21. Gratitude 22. Hope – optimism, future-mindedness, future orientation 23. Humour – playfulness 24. Spirituality – religiousness, faith, purpose	Strengths that forge connections to the larger universe and provide meaning

Exercise 3.1 Identifying your signature character strengths

Try to remember the last time when you felt extremely happy and engaged in an activity.

- How did it feel?
- What were you doing?
- Who else was involved?

Now, try to make a list of your signature strengths below:

If you have more time, go to the VIA® Institute web site and participate in the VIA Survey: http://www.viacharacter.org.

The VIA® Institute on Character was established as a non-profit organization in 2001 with the aim to advance the science and the practice of character strengths. It relates to the Authentic Happiness homepage of Dr Martin Seligman at the University of Pennsylvania, see http://www.authentichappiness.sas.upenn.edu/default.aspx.

The survey has 240 questions and it takes about 15 minutes. It results in showing your top strengths. List your signature strengths below:

Compare the list that you made earlier with the survey result; are they similar or different? Were there any surprises? Write your reflection below:

Knowing your SCS can help you to reach your full potential with your life – including work performance, family and social relationships.

Exercise 3.2 Using your signature character strengths

Now you have identified your SCS, how would you use more of your signature character strengths:

- In your life?
- With your family?
- In your social interactions?
- At work?

Consider the coaching questions:

- How did these strengths help you in the past?
- How will they help you in the future?
- How can you apply these SCS to your goal?
- How can you develop other strengths (those that are lower down on the list of your survey results)?
- Who can help further develop your SCS?
- How can you develop (reconfigure) your life and work such that they resonate more with your SCS?

As said, being fully aware of your own SCS and actively applying them to your life and work domains will increase your happiness. For instance, research has shown that cardiovascular patients who were experiencing positive emotions during the treatment period achieved greater and faster recoveries than those who did not experience positive emotions (Fredrickson *et al.*, 2000). Positive emotions seem to have a positive 'undoing effect' and this effect seems to occur across cultures. For further applications of positive psychology, see Hefferon and Boniwell, 2011; Kauffman and Scoular, 2004; Linley and Joseph, 2004a; Linley and Harrington, 2005.

Applying Learning to Coaching

In a way, strength-based coaching provides a vehicle for coaches to learn about aspects of their coachees and their 'self' that they might have taken for granted. Thus, one may argue that coaching in general provides the coachee with a learning environment and opportunities. For learning to take place, the coach needs to actively engage coachees in the learning process. This raises the following questions:

- What is the learning condition for coaching?
- How do you as a coach prepare the coaching environment and design the coaching process to optimize the coachees' learning experiences?
- What are the ingredients of this coaching–learning condition?
- What are the psychological, social and physical barriers for learning?

Exercise 3.3

If you have had experience of coaching as a coachee, try to recall your coaching session. Otherwise, think about your own learning experience, say, from school or college, for example the classroom, teachers and lecturers. Make a list of:

1. The negative experiences that may stand in your way for learning.
2. The attributes of a bad coach/teacher.
3. The attributes of a good coach/teacher.

From the above descriptions, try to answer the following questions:

What is the essence of learning?

____

____

____

____

What theories of learning do you know of that can explain this essence of learning?

____

____

____

____

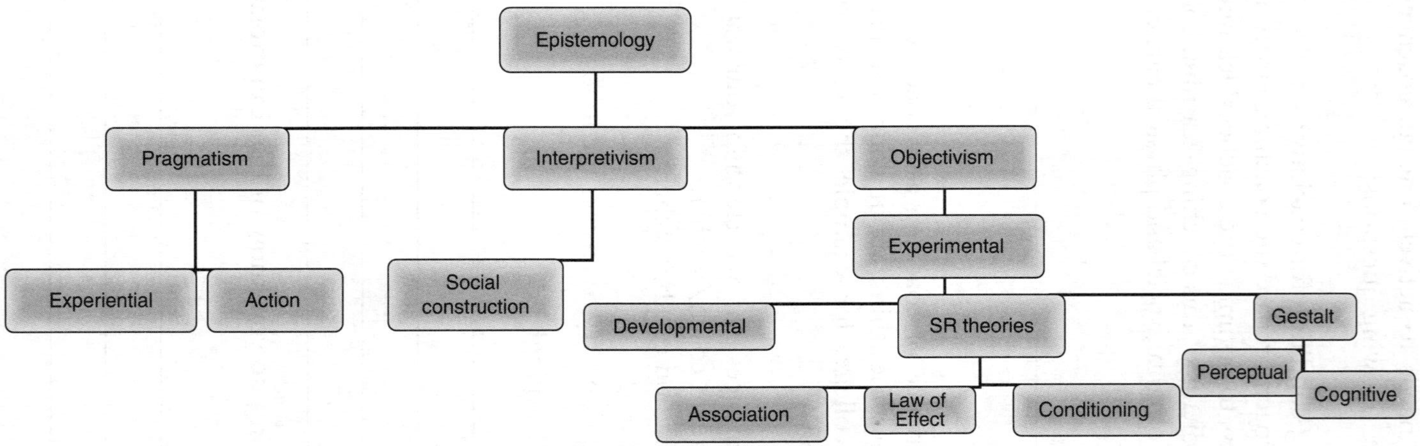

Figure 3.1 Taxonomy of learning theories

Psychology of Learning

Within the European tradition of studying psychology, learning theories can be classified in terms of epistemology and experimental approaches. The epistemological approaches consist of objectivism, pragmatism and interpretivism (Law, 2014). Within the experimental paradigm, there are four major learning theories: principle of association (Ebbinghaus, [1885] 1913); law of effect (Thorndike, 1874–1949); classical conditioning (Pavlov, 1849–1936); and gestalt theory. Figure 3.1 provides a taxonomy of these learning theories.

From the literature review, there are learning theories that are relevant to coaching (for example: Belenky *et al.*, 1986; Freire, 1992; Kegan, 1982; 1994, Kolb, 1984; Lave and Wenger, 1991; Loevinger and Blasi, 1976; Mentkowski *et al.*, 2000; Mezirow, 1991, 1996, 2000; Perry, 1970; Taylor, Marienau and Fiddler, 2000; Wenger, 1998). These include:

- the learning process
- reflective learning
- constructive-developmental theories
- social learning theories.

I shall highlight each in turn.

The learning process

Coaching, like learning, is a process that has a beginning, a middle and an end; and then starts something new all over again. This forms a cycle known as the learning cycle (Kolb, 1984). Figure 3.2 shows different stages of this cyclical process.

The learning cycle consists of four stages:

- Concrete experience – learners experience a situation that may present a problem or challenge.
- Reflection – learners take time to reflect upon their experience; this is an important part of the learning process (Merriam, 1994; Vaill, 1996) and coaching (Anderson, Knowles and Gilbourne, 2004).
- Abstract conception – learners need to make sense of what they have learnt and construct meaning.
- Action – learners need to undertake active experimentation to test the new concept that they have learnt.

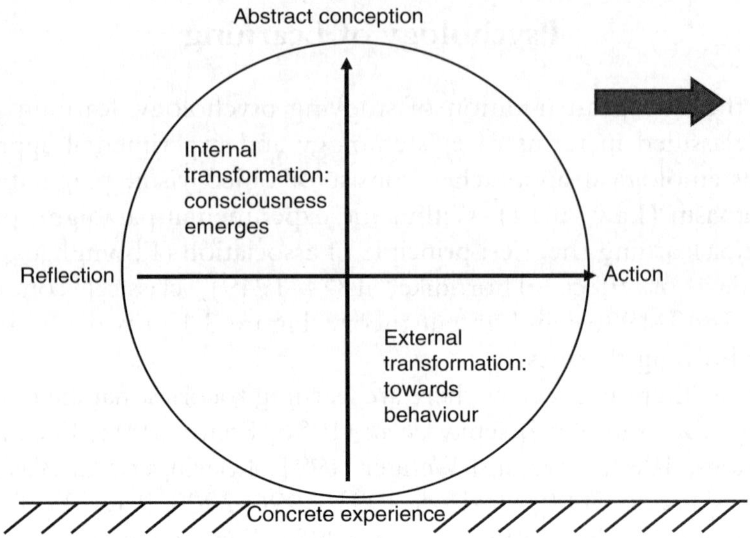

Figure 3.2 The learning wheel modified from Kolb's (1984) learning cycle

Table 3.2 Learning styles.

	Internal transformation	*External transformation*
Internal cognition	Thinker	Evaluator
External perception	Sensor	Actor

Exercise 3.4

Referring to Table 3.2, what is your preferred learning style?

What are the implications of the learning styles to your behaviour?

How do you know about the learning style of your coachee?

If you have identified the learning style of your coachee, how would you adjust your coaching to optimize the coachee's learning?

What are the strengths and weaknesses of each learning style?

What are the implications of the coachee's learning styles to coaching?

Some people are good at conceptualizing their learning (Thinkers), while others may readily experiment with their action plan (Actors). Some prefer learning from the actual experience (Sensors), while others like to take time to reflect upon their experience (Evaluators). Table 3.2 summarizes these four modes of learning styles.

The learning styles described earlier correspond to Honey and Mumford (2006):

- Actor – Activist
- Sensor – Pragmatist
- Evaluator – Reflector
- Thinker – Theorist

You can find out your own learning style by simply completing a Learning Styles Questionnaire (80 or 40 items: Honey and Mumford, 2000, 2006). However, very often, people seem to instinctively know about their learning preference and hence intuitively identify their own learning style (once they know what each style means). These are summarized as follows:

- Activists are ready to take action, like working with others and engaging in practical activities.
- Reflectors like to take time to think about the solution (pros and cons) before making a decision to take action.
- Theorists like to make sense of a situation (its meaning and purpose).
- Pragmatists like to apply theories into practice.

As you could understand from Exercise 3.4, each learning style has its strengths and weaknesses. In coaching psychology, we would like to develop ourselves and our coaches as *reflective practitioners* with an ability to achieve mastery of all four learning styles (Schön, 1983, 1991). I shall explore this further next.

Reflective learning

According to the learning cycle, we learn through reflection and action (*praxis*) and thereby develop new thinking and make informed decisions ('*conscientization*', Freire, 1992; '*emancipatory learning*', Brookfield, 1998; Jarvis, 1992; Mezirow, 1996). Reflection can be defined as:

> A cognitive process that involves both thinking and feeling about an experience (past or present) thereby a new consciousness emerges with a new appreciation, understanding and insight about that experience (Law, 2014; also see Brookfield, 1998; Boud, Keogh and Walker, 1985).

The reflection is a form of self-assessment. In coaching training, we often require our trainees to write a reflective account (coaching log) about their coaching practice as part of their continuous professional development. The format of a coaching log can be structured according to reflection stages of the learning cycle as follows (for example, see Gibb, 1988):

1. Description – describe what happened during the concrete experience.
2. Cognition and emotion – reflect on your thoughts and feelings. What were you thinking/feeling during the engagement/incident?
3. Analysis – try to understand what happened and draw meaning from the experience. What sense can you make of the experience?
4. Evaluation – assess the pros and cons, benefit and cost of the outcome of the experience.
5. Conclusion – summarize the meaning and lessons learned; look for improvement. In light of what happened, would you have done it differently? What else could you have done?
6. Recommendation/Action plan – recommend a future plan of action for further learning and improvement. If a similar situation arose again, what would you do? What are you going to do to further improve and develop yourself/your performance?

Figure 3.3 maps the above stages within the learning cycle. A template of such a reflective log is provided in the Appendix at the end of this book.

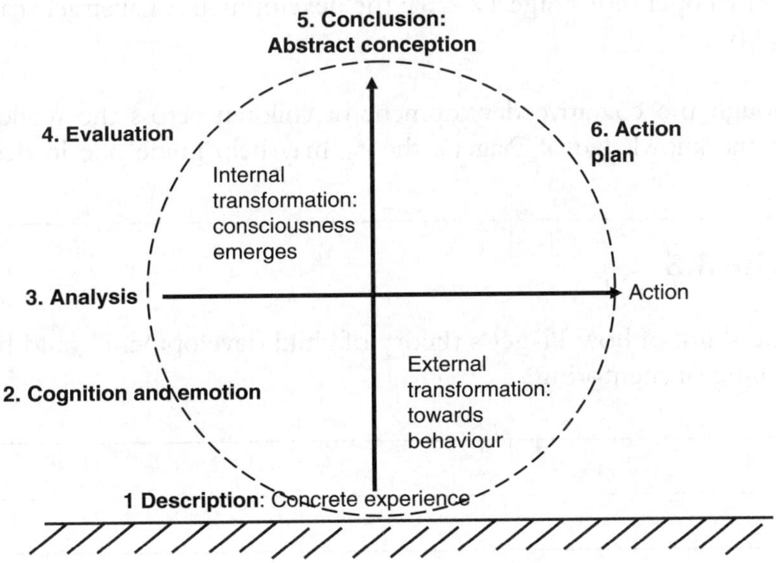

Figure 3.3 Six substages of reflection (combined models from Kolb, 1984 and Gibb, 1988)

Constructive-developmental theories

Constructive-developmental theories link the theory of learning to the human development and meaning-making processes (Belenky *et al.*, 1986; Kegan, 1982, 1994; Kohlberg, 1981; Loevinger and Blasi, 1976; Perry, 1970; Piaget, 1954). In this section, I shall focus on:

- Piaget's (1925–1980) stages of cognitive development in children and young people (Piaget, 1954).
- Levinson *et al.*'s (1978) stages of development in adults.
- Vygotsky's ([1926] 1962) social collaborative learning.

Piaget's theory of child development

Piaget (1954) proposed that the cognitive development of children consists of the following stages:

1. Sensorimotor (from birth–age 2): the development of sensory perception and the ability to respond via motor reflexes (e.g. grasping, sucking, manipulating objects to seek attention, imitating others' behaviour).
2. Preoperational (age 2–7): the development of linguistic and cognitive abilities for symbolic representation and imagination with the static and egocentric views of the world (from one's own perspective).
3. Concrete operations (age 7–12): the development of logical reasoning ability and multiple perspectives.
4. Formal operations (age 12–25): the development of abstract reasoning ability.

Although the cognitive development of children across the world varies greatly, the knowledge of Piaget's theory may help guide one in designing

Exercise 3.5

Can you think of how Piaget's theory of child development could be used in coaching or mentoring?

____

____

____

____

coaching and mentoring for parents and teachers, and interventions for children and young people (e.g. see Pask and Joy, 2007 and van Nieuwerburgh, 2012).

Levinson's life structure theory

Levinson *et al.* (1978) argue that the development does not stop in adulthood, and most people continue to develop cognitively throughout life. Using the metaphor of seasons, Levinson *et al.* (1978) proposed adults develop through the following stages:

1. Spring (childhood and adolescence: birth to age 20).
2. Summer (early adulthood: 17–40).
3. Autumn (middle adulthood: 40–65).
4. Winter (late adulthood: 60+).

The details of these life stages are summarized in Table 3.3.

Table 3.3 Stages of development in adults (adapted from Levinson *et al.*, 1978)

Life stages	
Title and age range	*Definition*
Early adult transition, 17–22 years	Establishment of independence, openness to new ideas, uncertainty about abilities
Provisional adulthood, 22–28 years	Proving of competence, especially to parents and oneself, gaining independence with own relationships
Age 30 transition, 28–33 years	Time of questioning commitments, individuals choose to change, leaving initial career choices and relationships
Time of rooting, 33–40 years	Culmination phase, reaping benefits of earlier career efforts. A consciousness of time sets in during this phase of life; people begin to settle down
Midlife transition, 40–45 years	Some people become tired of what they are 'supposed to be'. It represents a time of crisis for some. They may ask, 'Is this all there is to life?' Second round of questioning one's initial commitments
Restabilizaton/time of bearing fruit, 45–50 years	A time for inner development. One may mentor others, if one is established in a career. People at this stage seem to feel more settled
Age 50 transition, 50–55 years	Perception of belonging to 'another generation', reflective analysis of youthful dreams 'What did I/do I truly want from life?'
Middle adulthood, 55–60 years	This is a period of calm. People at this stage may begin disengaging from work. There is a sense that time is finite and relationships become more important
Late adult transition, 60–65 years	Stage of retirement for many and questioning how to structure the remaining years ahead

Exercise 3.6

Can you think of how Levinson's life structure theory could be applied to coaching?

____

____

____

____

Social constructive paradigm and cognitive-developmental theories – Vygotsky's zone of proximal development

By carrying out a number of systematic experiments which presented children with a set of tasks with various degrees of difficulty, Vygotsky ([1926], 1962, 1978) observed that children learn better when they are under guidance and working in collaboration with their peers. Vygotsky called the learning gap between an 'actual developmental level' and the higher level of 'potential development' the 'zone of proximal development'.

Exercise 3.7

What do you think about the idea of the 'zone of proximal development'? In what way is it relevant to your coaching context?

____

____

____

____

Coaching can be viewed as a form of social collaboration within which the coach provides coachees with support so that they can learn, develop and achieve their goal. In a way, using scaffolding as a metaphor, the coaching process provides the coaches with a structure such that they can scaffold across the zone of proximal development. The role of the coach here is to help the coachee to learn incrementally by designing a set of manageable (but challenging) tasks

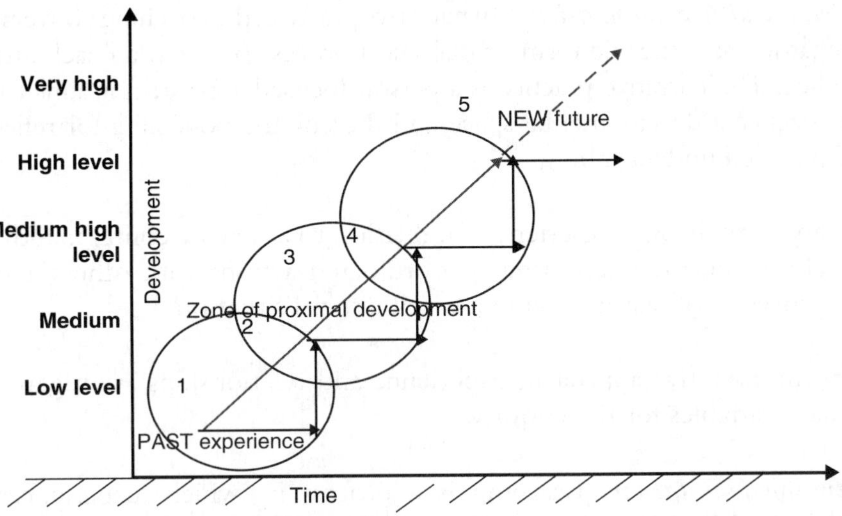

Figure 3.4 Zone of proximal development and the coaching/learning process

called 'distancing tasks' and support them to move forward from one zone of proximal development to the next. Figure 3.4 illustrates this process.

Vygotsky divided the development level (the vertical axis in Figure 3.4) into five levels with various amounts of complexity and difficulties:

1. Low level – simple tasks.
2. Medium level – relatively complicated tasks.
3. Medium high level – fairly complicated tasks.
4. High level – complex tasks.
5. Very high level – very complex tasks.

Vygotsky's learning theory and narrative coaching

Vygotsky's theory of learning scaffolding has been used in narrative therapy (White, 1997, 2000, 2006). Similar approaches used in narrative coaching have been independently developed by the author in the UK (Hall, 2006; Law, 2006a; Law, Aga and Hill, 2006) and Professor Reinhard Stelter in Denmark (Stelter, 2007, 2009; Stelter and Law, 2009, 2010). Other forms of narrative coaching have been developed separately by Dr David Drake (2006, 2007, 2008a,b, 2009) in Australia and the United States.

The narrative approach is grounded in two central foundations:

1. Societal/Cultural foundation – using reflection and cultural metaphors to help coachees to create meaning (e.g. Myerhoff, 1982; Turner, 1967).
2. Learning foundation – using Vygotsky's notion of proximal development to develop a community of practice.

Societal/Cultural foundation In narrative practice, the coaching conversation is regarded as a specific form of dialogical process between a coach and the coachee. The narrative practice is a person-focused approach; it aims to give the coachee a developmental space and thereby the possibility for reflection and renewed understanding:

i. about their own experiences in relation to a specific context; and
ii. about specific relationships, coordinated actions with others and the processes of negotiation in a specific social situation.

In the narrative approach, experience and relationships are regarded as primary variables for the enquiry.

Learning foundation Learning is a process by which 'experiences are transformed into knowledge' (Kolb, 1984: 38). Learning is based on the individual's curiosity and open-mindedness (zone of proximal development). It is influenced by the individual's experience from earlier and similar situations and therefore by specific expectancies about how to tackle new tasks and situations. Learning is qualified by a sharpened attention and consciousness in regard to the specific situation and concrete experiences. In the learning context, the learner develops a personal meaning and reflects values in regard to the given task/environment. Meaning comes from the individual's involvement and participation in practice.

Co-creation of meaning Social meaning-making always involves several people, the minimum being the dyad of coach and coachee or a group. Narrative techniques help coachees describe their life practice. There are various narrative techniques, depending on the coaching context (e.g. family, adults, children and young people). I would regard the key characteristics of the narrative practice as 'externalizing conversation' and 're-authoring methods'.

The concept of the externalizing conversation is that when coachees are telling the story about their life, very often they have internalized their 'problem' as if it were their own 'personal characteristic'. For example:

- Storyline: 'I performed badly …' (Problem: bad performance).
- Internalization: 'I am bad!'.

However, in narrative practice, the fundamental position is:

- The coachee/mentee is a person, not the problem.
- The problem is the problem itself (that is outside the person).

During the coaching session, learners experience a shift from gathering information into 'heaps', to developing complex chains of association (scaffolding). The zone of proximal development can be transversed via the sort of conversational partnership ('social collaboration') between coach and coachees and mentor and mentees. The coach provides the 'scaffolding' to help coachees to proceed across the zone of proximal development in manageable steps from the 'known and familiar' towards what might be 'possible to know'.

The coaching process can be regarded as collaborative learning in a form of narrative conversation. Through these engagements, all the participants redevelop the account of what they give value to and what they intend for their lives. This account can be regarded as concepts about their life and identity. The concept of development provides a foundation for people to develop a sense of personal agency, regulate their own lives and relationships, proceed with their lives, address their predicaments, overcome barriers to their aspirations and shape their existence in alternative ways.

The coaching or mentoring task is to contribute to the scaffolding of the proximal zone of development.

Social learning theories

Social learning theories (Lave and Wenger, 1991; Wenger, 1998, 2009) view learning as having the following characteristics:

- natural (part of human nature)
- meaningful (creating new meanings)
- experiential (socially situated)
- agency
- 'community of practice' with a social structure and pattern
- culture
- transformation (developing identity)
- developing collective histories
- boundaries (multiple forms of membership)
- social engagement with energy and power
- imagination
- alignment
- collectivity (social cohesion)
- spaces (within which conversations and learning can take place)
- citizenship (code of ethics that sustains commitment from participants)
- leadership (a key person who inspires other to learn as well as coordinates and manages the learning system or organization)
- governance (principles of 'governance' that guide the configuration of the system).

Exercise 3.8

Based on the social learning theories described above, consider the following questions:

- What kind of social experience constitutes learning?
- What kind of social interaction provides the optimal conditions for learning?
- What social context can best facilitate such interaction?
- What forms and structures enhance (rather than hinder) learning?

____

____

____

____

Applying Psychology of Learning to Develop a Coaching and Mentoring Framework

Three essential elements emerge from the review of learning theories; these are:

- experience
- reflection
- meaning.

We can combine the learning cycle (Figure 3.2) and the zone of proximal development (Figure 3.4) to produce a dynamic coaching model (Figure 3.5).

Referring to Figure 3.5, can you see the six substages of reflection described earlier within the learning cycle?

What is the missing link within the model so far?

Where do you think 'meaning' is created within the process?

Adding meaning-making as an intervening step in the cognitive (reflective) process in Figure 3.5, we have a more complete coaching–learning model (see Figure 3.6).

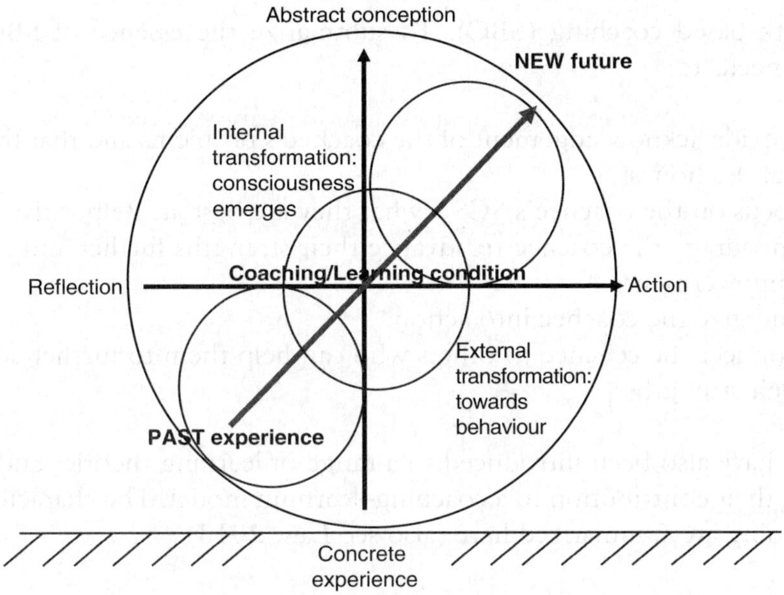

Figure 3.5 Model matching: learning cycle and coaching process

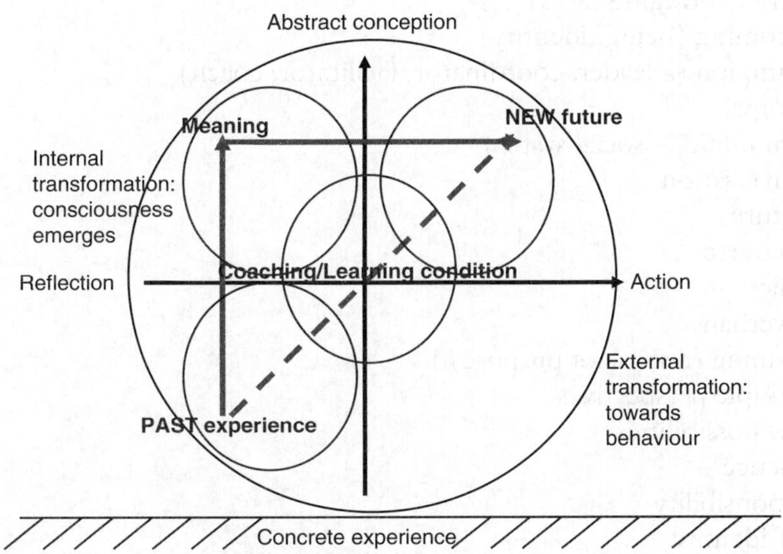

Figure 3.6 Dynamic coaching–learning model

Chapter Summary and Reflection

I started this chapter by first describing the development of positive psychology as a philosophical foundation for coaching, and the idea of using signature character strengths (SCS) for coaching – an approach known as strength-based coaching (SBC). To summarize the essence of SBC, the coach needs to:

1. Provide acknowledgement of the coachee's problems and that they are real. Be honest.
2. Focus on the coachee's SCS – what they are best at. Be positive.
3. Encourage the coachee to advance their strengths further and achieve empowerment.
4. Energize the coachee into action.
5. Connect the coachee to others who can help them to further advance their strengths.

You have also been introduced to a range of learning theories and identifying their contribution to a coaching–learning model. The characteristics of learning are summarized here (also see Law, 2013):

- action – doing (some social activities)
- awareness
- barrier (bridging tasks)
- becoming (being, identity)
- champion (a leader, coordinator, facilitator, coach)
- change
- community – social system
- conversation
- culture
- discourse
- ethics
- governance
- meaning (a sense of purpose)
- multiple perspectives
- new possibilities
- practice
- responsibility
- self-identity
- space

Can you add more to the above list?

4

Definitions

Coaching psychology, coaching, mentoring and learning

Introduction

This chapter provides a list of definitions of coaching psychology, coaching, mentoring and learning. However, before we start, it would be useful for you to think about it yourself and consider how you would define what coaching is:

- personally
- professionally (in theory and practice).

Also, consider the following questions:

- What are the similarities and differences between coaching psychology, coaching, mentoring and learning?
- Will the definition vary in different cultures?

Definitions of Mentoring and Coaching

People tend to think that a mentor is a person with more knowledge, experience and wisdom in the same field (e.g. career, or profession) as the mentee – the idea that a mentor is a trusted guide (Daloz, 1999), for example, Mentor in Homer's *Odyssey* and Confucius (孔子) in China. Many

Coaching Psychology: A Practitioner's Guide, First Edition. Ho Law.

practitioners draw a clear boundary between coaching and mentoring (e.g. Parsloe, 1992); while others do not (e.g. CIPD, 2012; Willis, 2005). I would argue that this is not necessarily true in the modern practice, and there is a lot of overlap between coaching and mentoring in terms of their skill base and model of practice.

Bob Garvey (2011) regards mentoring as a process of development. This may be psychological, social (Levinson 1997; Levinson *et al.*, 1978; Sheehy, 1977, 1996) and/or professional (Clutterbuck, 2004).

Exercise 4.1

Carry out an online search for definitions of mentoring and coaching. Try to include professional bodies in your search, for example:

- The Association for Coaching (AC), http://www.associationforcoaching.com/about/about03.htm.
- The Chartered Institute of Personnel and Development (CIPD), http://www.cipd.co.uk/hr-topics/coaching-mentoring.aspx#Informationpage.
- European Mentoring and Coaching Council (EMCC), http://www.emccouncil.org/src/ultimo/models/Download/102.pdf.
- International Coach Federation (ICF), http://www.coachfederation.org/.

From your search results, compare and contrast the characteristics between coaching and mentoring.

____

____

____

____

Now, summarize your results in terms of the following characteristics:

- Formality – Is the process formal or informal?
- Contract – What is the duration of the contract? Is it long term or relatively short term?
- Focus – What is the focus of the coaching or mentoring?
- Knowledge/experience – What kind of knowledge or experience does the coach or mentor require?
- Goal/agenda – What is the coaching/mentoring goal?

From my understanding, I have summarized my results in Table 4.1, which you can compare with yours.

Table 4.1 Similarities and differences between coaching and mentoring

Characteristics	*Coaching*	*Mentoring*
Formality	More	Less
Contract	Short term	Long term
Focus	Performance	Career/personal
Knowledge/experience	General	Specific
Goal/agenda	Dual	Single

Various scholars have captured the above essence in their definitions in one form or another. This can be summarized as follows:

- Facilitating the coachee's performance (Downey, 1999; Law, 2002; Parsloe, 1992; Whitmore, 2002).
- Unlocking people's potential (Law, 2002; Whitmore, 2002).
- Enhancement of learning and development (Downey, 1999; Parsloe, 1995; van Nieuwerburgh, 2012).

For the definition of coaching, I like to use the metaphor of a 'journey'. It resonates with the idea that a 'coach' is acting like a 'vehicle' which transports the coachee from A (where they are) to B (where they aspire to be in the future).

Exercise 4.2

There are diverse coaching styles (facilitation vs. instructional approaches). Which styles of coaching do you use (and why)?

How do these styles relate to the coachee's learning as well as your own?

How would you define learning?

____

____

____

____

Definition of Learning

As you have seen in Chapter 3, I argue that coaching should be grounded in the psychology of learning. Driscoll (2005) defines learning as a change in a person's performance or performance potential. What does this definition tell you about the learning process? And how does it relate to the learning cycle that you came across in Chapter 3?

Another way to look at the learning process is from the systems perspective (Figure 4.1). This consists of the following components:

- input
- means
- output
- outcome.

Exercise 4.3

Describe the ingredients of each of the above components:

Input: ____

Means: ____

Output: ____

Outcome: ____

How would you apply your learning to coaching?

____

____

____

____

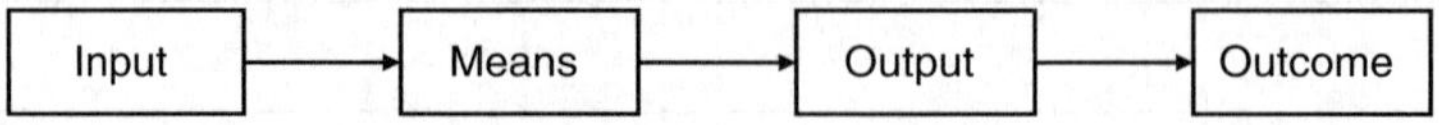

Figure 4.1 Defining a learning process

Definition of Coaching Psychology

You have defined coaching and identified the similarities and differences between coaching and mentoring. You have also learnt about how learning can be applied to coaching. So how would you define coaching psychology?

According to the BPS SGCP, coaching psychology is defined as:

> ... for enhancing well-being and performance in personal life and work domains underpinned by models of coaching grounded in established learning or psychological approaches (BPS SGCP, 2006: adapted from Grant and Palmer, 2002 and Palmer and Whybrow, 2006)

Proposal of a Universal Integrative Framework for Coaching Psychology

Law, Ireland and Hussain (2007) describe a universal integrative framework (UIF) for coaching as:

> Underpinned by psychological learning theory in a process that is developmental, brings about change and is culturally mindful. It enables flexibility and fluidity in its practice, to extend beyond boundaries.

It is proposed to examine the coaching practice along four dimensions:

1. personal
2. social
3. cultural
4. professional.

Exercise 4.4

You have considered a range of definitions of coaching, and its related concepts. Now make your own definition of coaching.

____

____

____

____

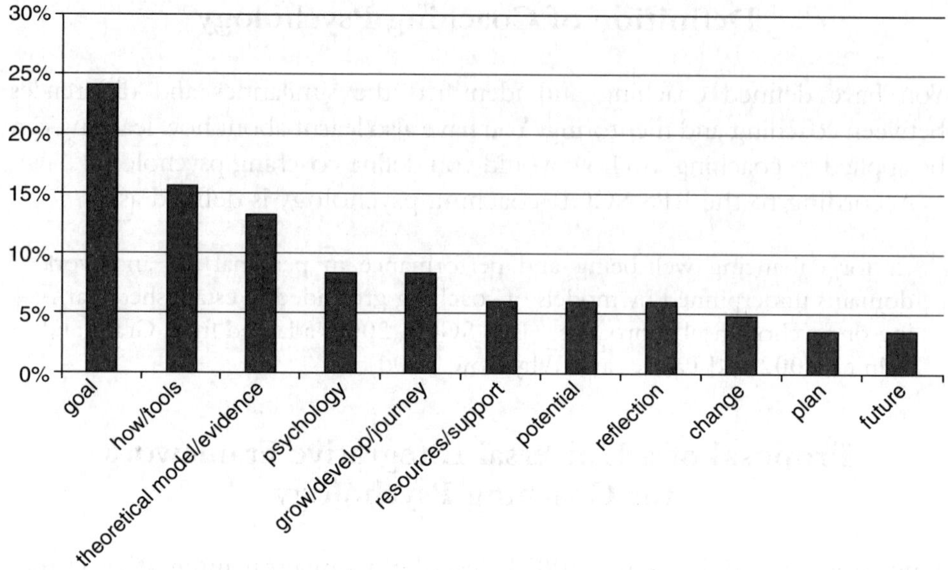

Figure 4.2 Definition of coaching

We shall explore these dimensions further in Chapter 6. For now it would be useful for you to consider each dimension. How would you develop your practice in coaching and learning?

I also ask the above question to applicants applying for the coaching programme at the university; over the years I have noted that the following items were most commonly mentioned (in order of frequency – see also Figure 4.2):

1. Goal – the skill to help the coachee to focus and achieve their goal.
2. How/tools – the coaching techniques.
3. Theoretical model/evidence – the theories and models that underpin coaching and are grounded in evidence practice.
4. Psychology – the psychology of coaching.
5. Grow/develop/journey – the skills to help coachees to grow and develop.
6. Resources/support – having resources to help coachees to unlock their potential.
7. Potential – help coachees to achieve and develop their potential.
8. Reflection – encourage coachees to consider past choices.
9. Change – the ability to change and help coachees to change their behaviour.
10. Plan – help coachees to plan their actions.
11. Future – skills to help coachees to focus on the future.

The above list shows that, in general, people who are interested in coaching (even though they may be untrained in the profession) already have a fairly good idea of what coaching is about and what they would expect to learn … so let's learn more …

Chapter Summary and Reflection

If you have read *The Psychology of Coaching, Mentoring and Learning*, you will notice that in that book, I advocate the idea of a coaching–mentoring continuum that is grounded in the psychology of learning, and its practice should be fluid, flexible and adaptable to different contexts and cultures. In this chapter we have considered the definitions of coaching and coaching psychology, and how they relate to other concepts such as mentoring and the theories of learning. The definitions embody the essence of coaching – the knowledge and skills that are required in coaching. You are invited to develop these skills further and practise more as we travel together along this coaching journey in the next few chapters.

5

Becoming a Learning Organization through Coaching and Mentoring

How do you introduce a coaching/mentoring programme into an organization?

Introduction

In Chapter 3, we reviewed some of the theories of learning and positive psychology, which forms a foundation for coaching. In Chapter 4, we reviewed a range of definitions about coaching and formulated our own definitions. In this chapter, we will expand our knowledge of coaching and apply it to the organizational context.

You will learn about the importance of developing a learning organization, how coaching can help to achieve the organizational goal, and the importance of developing a business case. You will also learn about the role of coaching within the context of organization and community, and the structures and components within it.

By the end of reading this chapter (completing all the exercises) you should be able to:

1. Recognize common challenges in organizations and explain how coaching can help.
2. Explain the role coaching can play in organizations and communities with a deeper appreciation of the role of culture and systems.
3. Understand different approaches to, and processes of, developing a business plan and strategy.
4. Explain how systems thinking may be used in developing a learning organization.

Coaching Psychology: A Practitioner's Guide, First Edition. Ho Law.

5. Describe the role and value of using psychometrics in coaching within the organizational context.
6. Critically review the role of leadership within organizations and communities.
7. Build an action plan for introducing coaching into an organization.

Challenges of the Changing World

Within the current economic climate, all businesses and organizations are under mounting pressure to increase efficiency and effectiveness and reduce cost and resources. There has been a growing number of

Exercise 5.1

Based on your own experience within an organization that you know (or a community group that you are part of), think about what changes the organization has been making, and list them below:

____

____

____

____

Have another look at the list of changes that you have written. Think about how those changes are related to the following aspects:

- leadership – including the competence of the leader (e.g. directors, managers and team leaders)
- new technology such as virtual social networking systems
- communication
- knowledge transfer
- complexity.

Then consider the following questions:

- What impacts would they have upon each item on your list?
- What kind of challenges did those changes aim to address?
- How successful were the changes in addressing those challenges?

outsourcing, mergers and collaborative partnerships in recent years. In order to gain a competitive edge in a bigger market place, there seems to be continuous restructuring, process re-engineering and re-organization.

Learning from case studies

In response to a changing world, organizations must continue to learn; and leaders need to adopt a new model of practice (Vaill, 1996; Lipman-Blumen, 1996, respectively). The following examples demonstrate the importance of learning.

From your reflection on the above exercise, it may have occurred to you that organizational culture, amongst many other things, is a key factor for the success or failure of business. As demonstrated by the two cases in Exercise 5.2, one shows an unethical corporate leadership culture, the other a hard to shift culture. The former operated unethical accounting and management practices which resulted in its chief executive on trial; while the latter held on to its traditional values and failed to respond to rapid changes in technology and the market. Indeed it is the value of the organization that seems to determine the organizational culture. Jan Thornbury (2000), a former consultant with KPMG, explains how a values-driven approach can revitalize a company culture. The lessons learnt from the case studies may include:

1. Changes present threats as well as opportunities – for example, in Case 2 the change in digital technology raised the challenges that threatened bankruptcy for one company while it created an opportunity for another company (e.g. Fujifilm) to diversify its products to embrace the change.
2. To successfully manage the change and leverage the opportunities that it presents, one needs to embrace change rather than be against it.
3. Successes of the past do not determine future success.
4. Value is a key determinant of the organizational culture.
5. The value needs to be ethical and the ethical principles need to be embedded in the management practice as part of the organizational culture.
6. Equality is an important value of a successful organization – this is characterized by perceived fairness, ownership and equal opportunities for all stakeholders to engage and contribute.
7. If the world is changing, the organizational culture needs to change, and so does its value.

Exercise 5.2

Read the following brief descriptions about the following companies. If you are not familiar with the actual cases of these companies (both made news headlines at the time), you may like to do some online research about them.

Case 1: Enron

In 2001 Enron Corporation (founded in 1985) had a stock market value of $35 billion and was the seventh largest US company on Fortune 500; but in 2006, it announced bankruptcy.

Case 2: Kodak

Eastman Kodak (formed in 1881) held 90 per cent of the market shares in photographic imaging equipment and film sales in the United States, and invested in the first digital camera in 1975; but in 2012, it filed for Chapter 11 bankruptcy protection.

What lessons have you learnt from the above two cases?

____

____

____

____

Why is it that some organizations have a winning culture, while others just have eye-rolling value statements?

So what makes the difference when it comes to values?

How should you go about defining the culture you want?

What should you do after you have proudly announced a value statement?

How can you change the organization's behaviour and other aspects of culture?

____

____

____

____

8. Successful organizational culture requires a purposeful engagement by all its members (employees), not just the senior management team.
9. An organization's ability to learn (including receiving customers' feedback) and change accordingly is important for its success.
10. The changing world calls for continuous re-evaluation and renewal of leadership and management practices; these practices need to be value-added and linked to improve the organization's performance and its increase in productivity (e.g. the manufacturing industry, see Koskela, 1992).
11. Any changes in organizational thinking, values and practices need to be communicated to all levels within the organization.
12. Leadership needs to be developed at almost all levels (not just the board of directors and the senior management team).

Meaning of change

The first learning point from the above section actually reflects the meaning of the word 'change'. Chinese words usually come in pairs; two words are used to describe the meaning more fully. The word 'change' in Chinese actually consists of two words: either 改變 or 變化

Each word has its own meanings:

改 – revise, rectify, correct
變 – change, transform, metamorphose
化 – melt, become, turn into, convert

Thus when the situation changes, it provides threats – structural transformations (as in metamorphosis) are imminent. At the same time, it also provides opportunities for action – to correct past wrongdoings, to rectify the situation, to revise the current situation and become something new.

Getting started

The first step to learn and develop any organization is to carry out a thorough business review of the organization (Verity, 2006). Typical approaches include SWOT and PESTEL analyses.

Exercise 5.3

Choose an organization (or a community group) that you are interested in and carry out SWOT and PESTEL analyses. Of course, if you are setting up or own a coaching company, you may wish to do this exercise on your own organization.

SWOT (Strengths, Weaknesses, Opportunities and Threats) – fill in Table 5.1.

Table 5.1 SWOT Matrix

Strengths:	**Weaknesses**:
Opportunities:	**Threats**:

PESTEL (Political, Economic, Social, Technological, Environmental and Legal aspects) – fill in Table 5.2.

Table 5.2 PESTEL Table

Political:	**Economic**:
Social:	**Technological**:
Environmental:	**Legal**:

Having identified the strengths and weaknesses of your organization as well as the opportunities and threats that it is facing (using PESTEL aspects), consider how you can help it to:

1. Become a competent organization in response to those aspects.
2. Become a learning organization in response to change.
3. Develop its leaders, to increase their professional competence, learning capacity, efficiency and effectiveness.

To answer the first question, you may also want to consider:

- What does a competent organization look like?

A Learning Organization is a Competent Organization

From my observation and literature review, a competent organization tends to have: the ability and resources to cope with the changing environment; a sense of direction; ethical values; satisfied stakeholders; and a long-term vision as well as short-term goals. These elements are usually formulated within the organization's strategy or business plan. Thus for any business (small or large, new or well established) it has to develop its strategy and business plan.

Strategy and Strategic Planning

A strategy ususally sets out the direction and scope of an organization, which helps it to fulfil stakeholder expectations and achieve advantage in response to changes in the market and environment (Johnson and Scholes, 1999). In general, to formulate and implement a strategy, an organization needs to carry out the following activities (see Hodgkinson and Sparrow, 2002):

1. Analysis of the environment and organization's strategic position.
2. Identifying the choice of options and courses of action.
3. Implementation of the strategy.

In relation to the above activities, there are three well-known approaches to developing a strategy in the business world:

- analytical (Porter, 1996)
- learning (Mintzberg, 1994)
- revolutionary (Hamel, 1996).

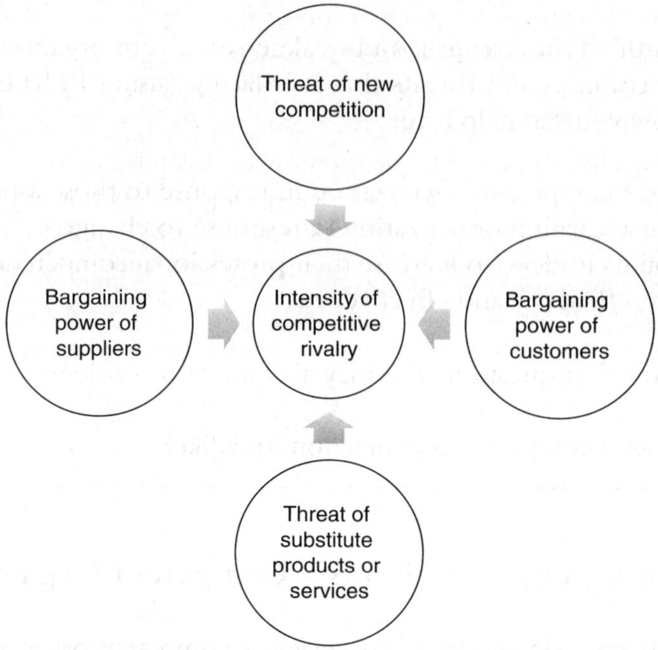

Figure 5.1 Porter's 5 Forces Analysis

I shall describe them in the following sections respectively.

An analytical approach to strategy development

Michael Porter (1996) regards developing a strategy as an analytical process. For Porter, the intensity of competitive rivalry is the major determinant of the organization's competitiveness within the market place. Thus, identifying one's own strategic positioning involves analyses of the competitive rivalry and its related forces of influences (see Figure 5.1):

- Threat of new competition – perfect competition (with zero profit) versus zero competition (maximum profit).
- Threat of substitute products or services – as in our example earlier, digital photography may make a good substitute for photographic film.
- Bargaining power of customers (the market of outputs) – customers have the power to put pressure on the organization. This may depend on the buyer and supplier concentration ratio, degree of dependency, availability of substitute products or services, price sensitivity and the uniqueness of the products or services.
- Bargaining power of suppliers (the market of inputs) – suppliers have the power to bargain for their charges when their resources are scarce.

- Intensity of competitive rivalry – increase in competition amongst other similar product and service providers.

Organizations may maintain their competitiveness through continuous learning, diversification and innovation rather than simply improving efficiency of production and cutting cost. Technological change could influence the consumer's behaviour – the increase in internet shopping is a good example. Thus, according to Porter, organizations need to have a strategy to maintain their competitiveness. This takes the following steps:

1. Analyse the market in the environment.
2. Identify your organization's strategic position that would give a positional competitive advantage.
3. Formulate the organizational policies according to its positioning.
4. Communicate the policies effectively throughout the organization.

A learning approach to strategy development

In Henry Mintzberg's (1994) view, changes are unpredictable. Thus any attempts at strategic planning would not help and may even impede strategic thinking. To make strategic decisions, leaders need to have a clear understanding of the following multi-facets (definitions) of strategy (the five Ps):

- Plan – define a plan of action.
- Ploy – define a specific manoeuvre to outwit competitors.
- Pattern – define a pattern of the behaviour.
- Position – define one's own organization's position in relation to the environment.
- Perspective – define the collective character (mindset) of the organization, as its perspective needs to be shared by all of its members.

A strategy that encompasses all of the above five Ps would only emerge through the organization's learning.

A revolutionary approach to strategy development

Gary Hamel (1996) regards strategy development as a revolutionary process. As such there are rule makers and takers as well as rule breakers who challenge the status quo. Like Mintzberg, Hamel believes that a strategy is something fluid and unpredictable. Thus, in addition to knowing one's own strengths and unique selling points in providing

Exercise 5.4

(a) In your view, which of the approaches to strategy is most useful to help leaders develop a strategic vision and manage change?

____

____

____

____

(b) If you are coaching a leader in an organization in response to change, how would you apply the approach that you have chosen in (a) and use it in your coaching conversation?

____

____

____

____

value-added services/products, organizations need to identify their core competences and continue to learn collectively, innovate and revolve.

To summarize, the three approaches to strategy development are based on:

1. rationality: analysis–choice–implementation process.
2. evolution or revolution
3. learning process.

As a coach, we need to help leaders of organizations to translate the organization's strategy into 'actionable knowledge' (term borrowed from Argyris, 1999). This can be achieved through organizational learning.

Organizational learning

To help develop a learning organization, the coach needs to help coachees within the organization to:

- *Learn* from experience (Argyris, 1977; Argyris and Schön, 1978; Cangelosi and Dill, 1965; Cyert and March, 1963; Garvin, 1993).
- Facilitate *collective* learning (Handy, 1989; Senge, 1990; Weick and Roberts, 1993).
- Increase knowledge which produces changes in attitude and behaviour and hence an *improved* outcome (Duncan and Weiss, 1979; Fiol and Lyles, 1985).
- Develop *routines* and procedures (Levitt and March, 1988).
- Manage *knowledge* (Blackler, Crump and McDonald, 1999; Staples, Greenaway and McKeen, 2001; Strata, 1989).
- Synthesize *shared understanding* (Ginsberg, 1990).
- Acquire useful *knowledge* and *change behaviour* (Huber, 1991).
- Generate knowledge by make tacit knowledge explicit (Nonaka, 1991).

Learning organizations are different from traditional resourced-based organizations in terms of the following task characteristics (Arvedson, 1993; Senge, 1990):

- Goal setting – shared visions instead of visions from the top.
- Thinking and doing – systemic (thinking and doing at all levels) rather than atomistic (the top thinks, the managers act).
- Conflict resolution – setting up dialogue, integrating diverse opinions, sharing understanding rather than mediating politically through a power relationship.

Knowledge and knowledge management

Exercise 5.5

One of the challenges for a learning organization is knowledge management. So what types of knowledge need to be managed within an organization? Spend 15 minutes thinking about the types of knowledge within the organizations that you are familiar with, and then make a list of them:

____

____

____

____

According to the literature review, there are five types of knowledge shared within an organization:

1. Dictionary knowledge (declarative knowledge) – declare *what* should be done (Sackmann, 1991, 1992; Zack, 1999).
2. Recipe (process) knowledge – procedure that describes how a specific task *should* be done (Cannon-Bowers and Salas, 1993; Sackmann, 1991, 1992; Zack, 1999).
3. Directory knowledge – how tasks are *actually* done (Rentsch and Hall, 1994; Sackmann, 1991, 1992).
4. People knowledge – knowing who knows what (Moreland, 2000).
5. Axiomatic knowledge (causal knowledge) – shared organizational attitudes, beliefs and values (the core part of organizational culture). It is this form of implicit knowledge that explains *why* the behaviour occurs (Mohammed, Klimoski and Rentsch, 2000; Sackmann, 1991, 1992; Zack, 1999).

Exercise 5.6

Identify what types of the above knowledge are explicit and which are tacit.

____

____

____

____

Learning Organization and Psychology of Learning

The five types of knowledge that I have summarized in the previous section can be learned and transferred from one person to another (as well as from one form to another) and constitute the overall organizational competence. Nonaka (1991) and Nonaka *et al.* (1996) identify four types of organizational competence:

- Socialization – people learn from each other (from tacit to tacit).
- Combination [integration] – explicit knowledge from different sources (organizational procedures, rules and processes) are combined to form a larger complex system (from explicit to explicit).

- Articulation – people communicate tacit knowledge explicitly (from tacit to explicit).
- Internalization – knowledge internalized in people's minds (from explicit to tacit).

These can be summarized in a knowledge transfer matrix as shown in Table 5.3.

The four types of organizational competence can be developed via the learning process between individuals within an organization. See Figure 5.2.

1. Socialization – people-to-people communication (experience).
2. Articulation – learning by doing (action).
3. Internalization via reflection and conceptualization.
4. Combination – automation (reflective experience or thinking in action).

Table 5.3 Knowledge transfer matrix (from Law, 2013)

Knowledge	*Implicit/Tacit–In people*	*Explicit–In process*
Implicit/Tacit–In people	**Socialization** (People–people)	**Articulation** (People–process)
Explicit–In process	**Internalization** (Process–people)	**Combination/ Integration** (Process–process)

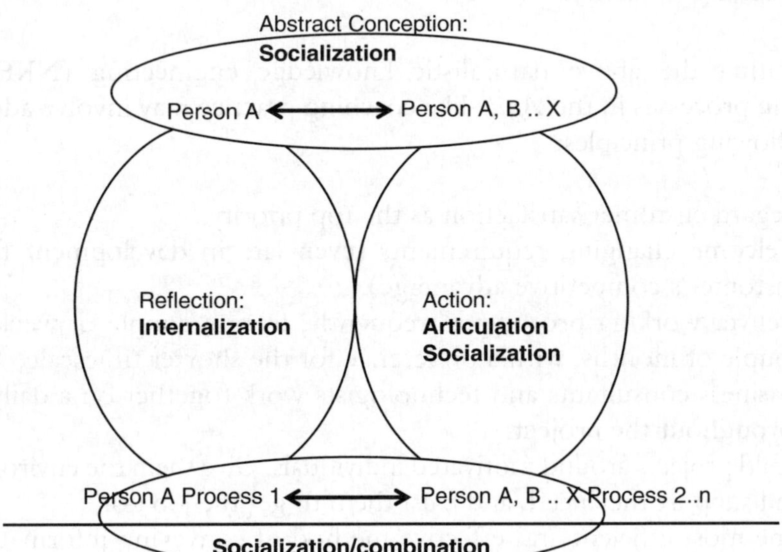

Figure 5.2 Learning cycles and knowledge network. Source: Law, 2014

The network model represents processes that resonate with:

- the cooperative inquiry (Heron, 1981a, b; Reason, 1988; Reason and Rowan, 1981)
- naturalistic or human inquiry (Bell and Hardiman, 1989; Lincoln and Guba, 1984)
- the *Agile* coaching approach (Davies and Sedley, 2009).

It consists of the following processes:

- Cooperative process – involves all stakeholders.
- Natural process – in the natural setting.
- Research process – an enquiry.
- Knowledge acquisition process (articulation) – knowledge transformation.
- Interactive process – experiential learning cycle (Kolb, 1984).
- Auditing process – validates the knowledge and procedures.
- Organizational process – context specific and sensitive to the organizational culture.

It involves the following activities:

1. Data collection and information gathering (concrete experience).
2. Reflection.
3. Abstract conception (or knowledge representation).
4. Planning for action.

Integrating the above naturalistic knowledge engineering (NKE) and learning processes in the *Agile*-like coaching practice may involve adopting the following principles:

1. Regard customer satisfaction as the top priority.
2. Welcome changing requirements (even late in development for the customer's competitive advantage).
3. Deliver working prototypes frequently, from a couple of weeks to a couple of months, with a preference for the shorter timescale.
4. Business consultants and technologists work together on a daily basis throughout the project.
5. Build projects around motivated individuals. Give them the environment and support they need, and trust them to get the job done.
6. The most efficient and effective method of conveying information to and within a development team is face-to-face conversation.
7. The working prototype is the primary measure of progress.

8. *Agile* processes promote sustainable development. The sponsors, developers and users should be able to maintain a constant pace indefinitely.
9. Continuous attention to technical excellence and good design.
10. Keep things simple.
11. Develop self-organizing teams.
12. Continuously strive for improvement – at regular intervals, the team reflects on how to become more effective, then tunes and adjusts its behaviour accordingly.

See http://www.agilemanifesto.org/principles.html.

Leadership and Organizational Coaching

Role of the top team

Exercise 5.7

From reading about the strategic planning, knowledge management, learning organizations and their competence so far, what do you think the role of the top team should be? Make a list below:

____

____

____

____

You can probably see the importance of the top team in terms of ensuring knowledge is managed and transferred throughout the organization and its learning and performance. So what does the top team of a learning organization look like? How many people? What are the skills, knowledge, experience and cultural mix in terms of its team members?

Previous research has been done by many scholars on the above questions (see Chattopadhyay *et al.*, 1999; Lioukas and Chambers, 1998; Markoczy, 1997; Miller *et al.*, 1998; Murray, 1989; Smith *et al.*, 1999; Sutcliffe and Huber, 1998; Wiersema and Bantel, 1992). Law *et al.* (2007) and Law (2014) summarized the findings and suggested that there is 'an optimal level of diversity' for the top team, and its relationship to organizational performance is an inverted U-shape curve (Figure 5.3).

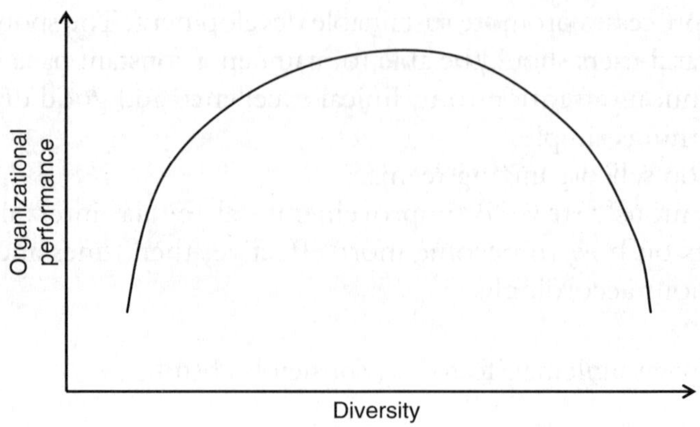

Figure 5.3 Organizational performance versus top team diversity. Source: Law, 2014

Exercise 5.8

Given the diversity and organizational performance relationship as shown in Figure 5.3, how would you coach company directors who wish to develop their senior management team to achieve a high performance? If you also coached individual members of the team, how would you help them to have shared visions, beliefs and values? What does the top team look like? What are the characteristics of a leader in the top team? What are their core competences? How would they lead the team? What are their leadership styles? As a coach, how would you develop their leadership styles?

____

____

____

____

Again, research has shown that there is no single leadership style that would be suitable for all situations. To be effective, leaders would need to adopt a range of leadership styles (three or four different styles) to apply to different situations and individuals as appropriate (Fitzsimmons and Guise, 2010). Common leadership styles include:

- Affiliative – ensure a good working relationship between team members.
- Authentic – with a personal charisma and genuineness.
- Coaching – improve employees' performance in alignment with the organizational objective.

- Directive – command action.
- Transformational – energize people into action with a sense of purpose.
- Inspirational (visionary) – inspire team members to move forwards.

Jean Lipman-Blumen (1996) advocates the so-called Connective Leadership Model and that leaders need to learn and adopt more relational and instrumental leadership skills in managing diversity. The Chartered Management Institute (CMI) defines leadership in terms of the following qualities:

1. Leading people.
2. Meeting customer needs.
3. Managing change.
4. Managing information and knowledge.
5. Managing projects, processes and resources.
6. Managing yourself.

Exercise 5.9

Compare the CMI core competences for leadership with Lipman-Bluman's Connective Leadership Model (see http://www.achievingstyles.com/asi/achieving_styles.asp), identify which leadership styles are more suitable in each area of competence and under what situation. Develop your own leadership model from the leadership styles and competence. As an executive coach, how would you apply such a model (of competence–leadership style) in your own practice?

____

____

____

____

Psychometrics in Organizations

From Exercise 5.9, how do you find out about your coachee's preferences in order to adopt certain leadership styles? In the exercise, you may have covered the use of psychometric assessments as proposed by various scholars (Law, 2014; Passmore, 2009). Psychometric assessment may be used to help the coach to:

- Identify the areas of development that the coachee may need.
- Understand the coachee's personality.
- Increase the coachee's awareness.
- Match the coachee's strength with their role within the organization.
- Provide the coachee with feedback about themselves, their areas for development and help develop an action plan.

Exercise 5.10

Think about your coaching session. How would you help your coachees to become aware of their own strengths and preferences? How would you help them to discover their area for further improvement in order to fulfil their current or future roles?

____

____

____

____

In this section we shall consider more about the use of psychometric instruments in leadership coaching and their implications. For example, a coachee's transformational leadership styles can be assessed by ELQ™ (Alimo-Metcalfe and Pritchett, 2008) and their mental toughness can be measured by MTQ48 (Clough and Strycharczyk, 2012). I shall briefly describe these in turn.

Bernard Bass's (1985) transformational leadership style has been very popular in recent years. The ELQ is a useful 360-degree feedback tool designed to assess a coachee's transformational leadership style. It assesses coaches in terms of the following aspects:

1. showing genuine concern
2. being accessible
3. enabling
4. inspiring others
5. building a shared vision
6. supporting a development culture
7. facilitating change sensitively
8. acting with integrity

9. being honest and consistent
10. encouraging change
11. networking
12. resolving complex issues
13. being decisive
14. focusing team effort.

The model of mental toughness also relates to resilience (Dyer and McGuiness, 1996) and hardiness (Kobasa, 1979). It describes behaviours and outcomes associated with tough-minded people in terms of four dimensions:

- control
- challenge
- commitment
- confidence.

This tool (MTQ48) may be useful for coaches to assess their coachees who are working in a stressful, changing or challenging environment; and how to identify and cope with those challenges. However, is having the quality of mental toughness enough to be an effective leader? What are the areas for development for mentally tough leaders? A tough-minded leader may have a risk in bullying others as part of their drive for control, commitment and confidence; they may be perceived as insensitive, intolerant and unforgiving (Clough and Strycharczyk, 2012). Thus other assessments and developments may be necessary even for those leaders who score well in the MTQ48 assessment. Table 5.4 provides a summary of other common psychometric instruments in the market that you may find useful for your coaching practice.

Table 5.4: Common psychometric instruments

Tools	*Measurement*
OPQ32	Dimensions of personality that are specifically relevant to job performance
Wave	Big Five model of personality
Neo	Big Five model of personality
HDS	'Dark Side' of personality (Hogan Development Survey)
MBTI	Four personality types: • Extravert – Introvert. • Sensing – Intuitive. • Feeling – Thinking. • Perceiving – Judging.
16PF	16 major dimensions of personality

Developing a Coaching Culture

So far we have argued the importance of developing a learning organization and how coaching can help leaders to develop themselves in relation to this. Apart from individual development and considering an organization as a whole, how would you help an organization to develop a learning culture?

Unsurprisingly, developing coaching may be our answer. How do we know that an organization has a coaching culture?

Exercise 5.11

Think about an organization that you know, or imagine a hypothetical one – what is a learning organization like? Make a list of its characteristics:

____

____

____

____

A learning organization with a coaching culture means that its members are likely to have:

1. a commitment to develop the learning capacity of its employees
2. non-directive leadership styles
3. a passion
4. a clear goal
5. good team relationships
6. autonomy
7. value learning.

And the organization as a whole tends to have:

1. an atmosphere of openness, recognition and respect
2. a learning environment
3. 360-degree coach and mentor processes in place
4. competent teams
5. regular performance reviews
6. collective recognition and rewards in teams
7. coaching and learning practice embedded.

(See Chaplain, 2003; Hardingham *et al.*, 2004; Megginson and Clutterbuck, 2005; Law, 2014.)

Exercise 5.12

Given the above list of characteristics, who do you think should be a key person to develop such a culture? (See Law, 2014; Wenger, 2009.)

____

____

____

____

Exercise 5.13

If you were asked to introduce a coaching programme in an organization, and to put forward a business case, how would you set out to do that?

____

____

____

____

A typical business case may consist of:

- strategic elements – aims with SMARTER (i.e. Specific, Measurable, Agreeable or Achieving, Realistic, Time bound, Evaluable and Reviewable) objectives
- economic arguments – cost and benefit/effectiveness
- financial viability
- commercial aspects
- project management plan.

(See Law, 2014 for further details.)

Exercise 5.14

Having won the case for introducing a coaching programme into an organization, how would you embed coaching culture within it?

____

____

____

____

Hawkins and Smith (2006) suggest the following steps:

1. Introduce individual coaching for a few members within the organization.
2. Develop organization-wide coaching and mentoring programmes.
3. Support coaching initiatives.
4. Embed coaching as part of HR and performance management function.
5. Developing coaching as part of leadership styles and management competence.
6. Continue to learn and consolidate the learning culture.

Figure 5.4 summarizes the process.

In summary, developing a learning culture and embedding good coaching practice within it requires the following:

1. leadership development
2. social support
3. coordination
4. collaborative partnership
5. learning communities.

A learning culture can only be sustainable when all stakeholders embed a learning process in their work in mutually beneficial ways. Developing a community of practice is an important aspect; we shall focus on this next.

Communities of practice are communities with a collection of individuals (members) who are in pursuit of a common goal through their interactions, where they learn about the rules of engagement and develop skills and

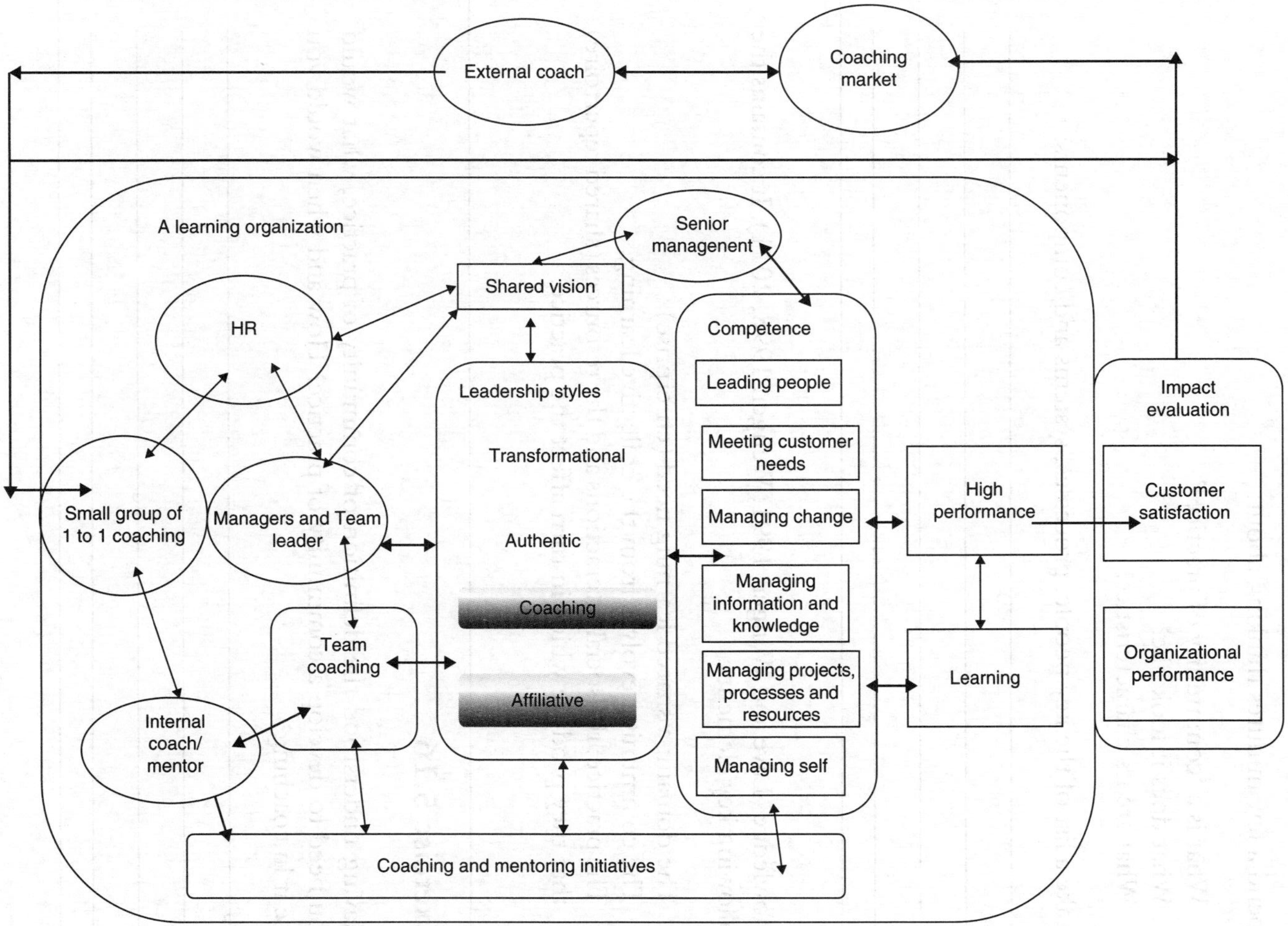

Figure 5.4: Developing a coaching culture. Source: Law, 2013

Exercise 5.15

Spend a few minutes thinking about:

- What is a 'community of practice?'
- What does it look like?
- What are its characteristics?

Make a list of the key people, processes, systems and components:

____

____

____

____

knowledge (Lave and Wenger, 1991; Wenger, 1998, 2011). It contains the following key elements:

- The domain: a shared learning need (enterprise).
- The community: evolves from the collective learning.
- The practice: the social interactions and the resources (shared repertoire) that they produce which in turn affect the practice.

Exercise 5.16

Having understood the definition of community of practice, what would you need to develop a community of practice? How and when would you use it in coaching?

____

____

____

____

Wenger (1998, 2011) proposed that developing a community of practice needs the following:

1. social learning spaces
2. learning citizenship
3. social artists (a key coordinator)
4. learning governance.

Chapter Summary and Reflection

In this chapter, you have learnt about coaching within the context of an organization and how coaching can be introduced and embedded within it. We have discussed the importance of organizational culture and how a learning culture may be maintained. To sum up, a learning organization consists of:

- Input – experience.
- Process – routines and procedures that allow people continuously to learn.
- Output – behaviour, products and services, action, and history.
- Outcome – shared understanding and *values*, expanded capacity, improved competences and customer satisfaction.

To develop yourself as a coach, you will need to develop yourself with the following competences:

- awareness
- empathy
- understanding different personality dimensions of yourself and your coachees
- diplomacy
- facilitation skills
- learning skills
- listening skills
- management of change
- tolerance of ambiguity.

In the next few chapters, I shall show how the above competences can be further developed.

6

GROW Model and Universal Integrative Framework

Build your own model and apply it

Introduction

In Chapter 5 you learnt that coaching can act as a vehicle for developing an organization. In this chapter, I shall introduce a coaching framework from the personal and organizational as well as cultural perspectives. This is based on the learning theories that were described in Chapter 3. From the framework, I hope you will have some ideas about building your own model of coaching.

By the end of reading this chapter (completing all the exercises) you should be able to:

1. Understand the coaching and mentoring process using the GROW model.
2. Understand the importance of self, social, cultural and professional dimensions within the Universal Integrative Framework (UIF) and outline their roles in coaching/mentoring.
3. Develop your own coaching model as appropriate.

Theories, Model, Techniques and Skills

I have been teaching coaching and coaching psychology for some years now. From my experience/observations, many students have difficulties differentiating between theories and models and their applications

Coaching Psychology: A Practitioner's Guide, First Edition. Ho Law.

(techniques/tools and skills). So to clarify these concepts, I shall explain these in this section. But first, please spend 10 to 15 minutes thinking about what these terms actually mean.

Exercise 6.1

What are a theory, a model and a technique?

Define each concept in your own words, based on your understanding:

A theory is: ______________________________

A model is: ______________________________

A technique is: ______________________________

____

Give an example for each term

____

____

____

____

To me, theories and models are two different things. A model is merely an abstract simplified description or representation of a complex system. It is a concept to show the essence of how the system works. Having a model for your coaching can guide you in articulating what to do. It also enables you to provide a rationale to account for your actions (should you be required to do so by your coachees, customers or supervisors). Using our 'journey' metaphor, it provides you with a map to help your coachees to understand where they are going and how you are helping them. The popular GROW model is an example which provides you with a description of the different stages of the process.

A theory, in a scientific sense, refers to a proposed explanation of empirical phenomena (a causal relationship, e.g. $Y = aX1 + bX2 + C + e$) that either has already been tested or can be tested experimentally. Models are very difficult to test. Examples of theories are Kelly's personal construct theory and learning theories (e.g. classical and operant conditioning) in Stimulus–Response (S-R) psychology.

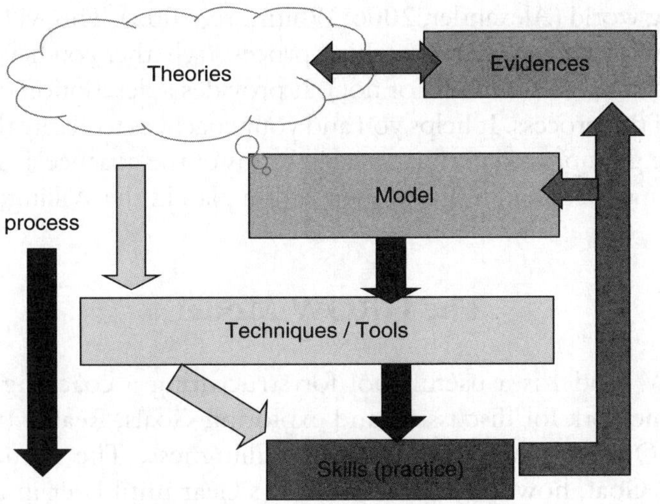

Figure 6.1 Theories, model, techniques and skills

When applying theories into your coaching practice, it is here that you can draw on the techniques that are embodied in the model. Again students often get confused between techniques and models. A technique is a very specific set of procedures (often step by step) which is based either on a theory (which provides a formulation) or embedded in a model (which provides a framework/structure). For example, the dream work is in a psychodynamic model; the repertory grid technique is in personal construct theory; the Myers-Briggs Type Indicator (MBTI) is based on Jungian theory; meditation/mindfulness procedures are based on gestalt psychology; cognitive behaviour therapy (CBT) on cognitive and behavioural psychology. Figure 6.1 illustrates these differences and the inter-relationship between theories, models and techniques.

From the above clarification, it is easy to understand the attraction of building your own model of coaching or a generic framework. Having a generic framework of coaching (a meta model) has the following benefits (Lane, 2005):

- Structure – it provides you with structure to guide your coaching process and relate to other models of coaching.
- Questions – it helps you to ask appropriate questions according the process of the model.
- Leadership – it gives coaching a sense of direction.

In this chapter, I shall describe a version of such a framework (sometimes called a meta model). But first I shall briefly describe a typical coaching model – the GROW model as it is widely known and practised in the coaching world (Alexander, 2006; Whitmore, 2002). This will help you to become familiar with a general coaching process (whether you have previously come across the GROW model or not). It provides a description of the different stages of the process. It helps you and your coachees to clarify the expected outcomes (e.g. improved performance in terms of the coachee's Goal, or specific behaviour change in terms of their action plan in the Willingness stage).

The GROW Model

The GROW model is a useful tool for structuring a coaching session. It offers a framework for discussing and exploring Goals, Reality (the current situation), Options and Way forward/Willingness. The natural starting point is the Goal, however, this isn't always clear until later in the session, so it may need revisiting later. Although it seems a linear structure, it is a reiterative/circular process such that the Goal set can be reviewed in future sessions. After discussing the Way forward it may be necessary to revisit the Options, or realign the Goal.

A typical GROW coaching session

We can design a coaching/mentoring session or even a whole programme according to the GROW model. The first stage is to focus on setting the Goals; then check the Reality in terms of the current situation. Possible Options are then explored. Finally a Way forward is agreed. In practice, we would find that it is not that easy to identify the Goals without setting the context (topic) or reviewing the current situation (Megginson and Clutterbuck, 2009). Hence the GROW model may sometimes be referred to as TGROW (where T stands for Topic). In practice, coaches/mentors need to be flexible in terms of the ordering of the stages in the process – moving to and fro between each stage as necessary.

Goals

According to GROW, the first stage of coaching/mentoring is to understand the coachee's goals, aims and/or objectives.

Your questions may include:

- What are your hopes and dreams (the bigger picture, long term)?
- What do you hope to achieve (in the short, medium or long term)?
- What do you want to accomplish at the end of this session (immediate term)?
- What are your expectations of coaching/mentoring (about the process itself)?

Exercise 6.2

What questions would you ask the coachees at the Goal stage?

In eliciting the coachee's hopes and dreams, the questions asked need to help the coachee in clarifying and consolidating their aspirations so that a SMART or SMARTER goal/objective can be formulated.

SMARTER is an extension from the SMART acronym (Doran, 1981). It stands for:

- Specific.
- Measurable.
- Achievable/agreeable.
- Realistic/relevant.
- Time bound.
- Evaluation.
- Review.

Useful questions include:

- Specific: What does 'good' look like (e.g. in terms of work/life domain)? How will you know when you get there (the journey metaphor)?
- Measurable: How do you measure your success/progress?
- Achievable/agreeable: Is it achievable? Would your parents/line manager/team agree with this?
- Realistic: How realistic is this ambition?
- Time bound: When by?
- Evaluation and Review: When would you like us to meet again and review this? How do you know it is effective? How do you measure the benefits of achieving this?

According to research (Locke and Latham, 1990), goal setting is an important factor for success. Thus goal setting can make a crucial difference to the coachee/mentee in terms of achieving a desirable outcome.

The goal needs to be challenging as well as realistic. If it is too difficult, it becomes unachievable; too easy and it can be uninteresting. Either case could have a de-motivating effect upon the coachee.

Breaking a large ambitious vision (a more long-term goal) into a set of inter-related smaller sub-goals may be desirable. This helps monitor progress, and sustain motivation (Lerner and Locke, 1995).

Also, please remember it is the coachee's/mentee's dream, thus the goal belongs to the coachee/mentee (and no one else). This increases the coachee's/mentee's commitment. The coachee/mentee is the owner of the goals and should take the responsibility of achieving them (Gollwitzer, Heckhausen and Ratajczak, 1990), though other stakeholders may be involved along the way.

Reality

The reality check allows the coachees/mentees to re-evaluate their current situation and thereby identify the gap between where they are and where they want to be. In coaching, this may involve reviewing their past and present performances that are relevant to their goal, and establish track records (including 360-degree feedback from others if available).

Exercise 6.3

What questions would you ask the coachees at the reality stage?

____

____

____

____

Typical questions may include:

- What is the current situation?
- What have you done so far in relation to this? Can you give me some examples?
- What are the barriers?
- How do you feel about your achievement so far?

Options

This stage consists of two parts. During the early part of the options stage, you should be as creative as possible (with a non-critical, non-judgemental attitude) to generate the maximum number of options. This opens up a whole world of possibilities that the coachees may not have thought of before.

There are various tools and techniques to help the coachee generate a list of options, for example: Buzan's (2000) mind mapping; Crawford's (1954) attribute listing; de Bono's (1970, 1985) six thinking hats and random words; and Osborn's (1948) brainstorming.

Exercise 6.4

What questions would you ask the coachees at the options stage?

____

____

____

____

The questions may include:

- What are the options?
- What have you not tried before?
- If you could do anything, what would you do?
- Finally, please give me one more idea.

The second part of the option stage is about decision making. While the early part of this stage was about opening up new possibilities, this part is about narrowing it down to a finite feasible set of options in terms of their feasibility. This enables the coachees/mentees to decide which options are most realistic and likely to be achieved.

Questions include:

- Let's look through this list of options one by one. What are their pros and cons?
- Is this feasible?
- How much would this cost?
- How long would this take?

Way forward (or Willingness)

At the final stage of the GROW model, the coach/mentor and coachees/mentees usually agree a way forward and generate an action plan that links to the selected options as the output of the session. The coach/mentor should also check to see if the coachees/mentees are committed to take the plan forward and whether there are any barriers that may prevent them from achieving those actions.

Exercise 6.5

What questions would you ask the coaches at this stage?

____

____

____

____

Questions may include:

- Can you summarize the key points that we have agreed in this session?
- What are you going to do?
- What are the possible barriers?
- How would you overcome them?
- Who could help you to overcome those barriers?
- What support/resources do you need?
- Who needs to be involved?
- How do you get there?
- When by?
- When shall we review this?

The Universal Integrated Framework (UIF)

The Universal Integrative Framework (UIF) was initially developed by Law, Ireland and Hussain, (2007) through their coaching practice in health and social care in the UK, and multinational programmes involving African, Asian, Chinese and European businesses. It was further developed and expanded by Law (2014). In addition, Goleman's (1995, 1998) work on emotional intelligence focuses on the cultural competence that is applicable across cultures. The model is a pragmatic meta model with the following unique characteristics:

1. Appreciation of a cultural environment – the framework emphasizes the significance of appreciating others' cultures as well as one's own. It encourages the coach and coachees to understand that culture is multi-layered and that culture exists in all coaching situations.
2. Coach/coachee fluidity – the framework views both coach and coachee as learners (and experience has shown that very often

the coach learns more than the coachee in a coaching process). Thus both coach and coachee may benefit from learning about coaching and act as a coach/coachee or mentor/mentee in different contexts. This would enable them to acquire the knowledge of the whole coaching system and recognize the learning opportunities in both roles. It would help them to identify the roles as transitory, to aid learning rather than as set and 'boxed-in' positions.

3. Integrative continuum – the framework regards coaching and mentoring as an integrative continuum. In other words, it views coaching and mentoring as interchangeable practices. Both share a similar set of skills. It implies that, very often, it would be beneficial for the mentor to learn about coaching models; and sometimes, it may be important for a coach to learn a new domain of knowledge so that they can understand their coachee's business/professional context better.
4. Continuous professional development (CPD) – it integrates CPD and supervision within the coaching process. The framework provides opportunities for both the coach and coachees to review their learning together – moving from 'I-learning' to 'we-learning'.
5. Communication methods and feedback mechanism – the UIF offers a 360-degree feedback mechanism. This assesses the perspectives of coaches and coachees, and provides them further opportunities to become aware of their competence and identify areas for development.
6. Cultural social intelligence – the framework consists of an online tool that measures the coach's or coachee's cultural and social competence (CSC) as well as the personal and professional competences (i.e. four dimensions).

To summarize, broadly speaking, the UIF consists of four dimensions.

1. Personal competence.
2. Social competence.
3. Cultural competence.
4. Professional competence.

The structure of the framework is shown in Figure 6.2.

The above conditions are linked to the coach's/mentor's and/or coachee's/mentee's competence. As said, the four dimensions of the coaching competence (CSC) have been developed as an online tool in a form of self-review questionnaire (SRQ); it consists of 100 questions which assess the individual's coaching competence along those four dimensions. Readers who are interested in trying out the CSC SRQ can contact the author (see contact point in the Preface). The four dimensions with their 18 elements are described in detail in Law (2014). For the benefit of the reader, these are summarized below.

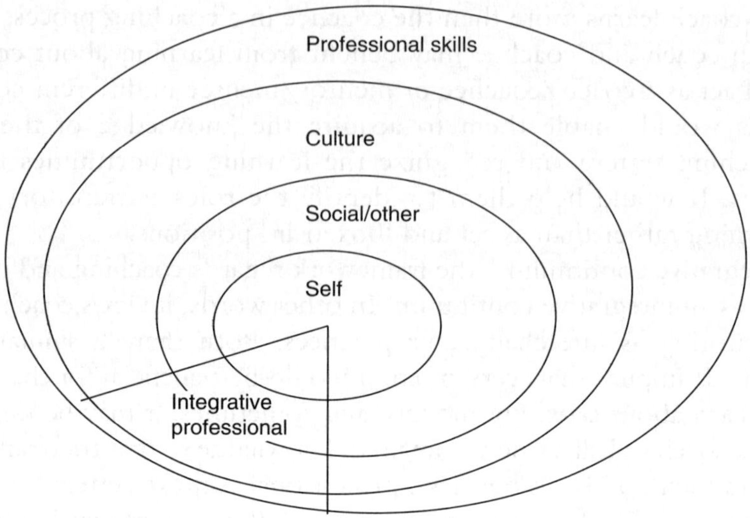

Figure 6.2 The Universal Integrated Framework. Source: Law, Ireland and Hussain, 2007; Law, 2013

Dimension I: Personal competences

These competences reflect how we manage ourselves. They consist of two parts:

- Awareness of oneself (self-awareness).
- Management of oneself (self-regulation/self-management).

Awareness of oneself (self-awareness)
Measures whether you accept and value yourself. Awareness of one's own internal states, feelings, emotions, cognition, preferences, resources and intuitions.

Element 1: Emotion Awareness of your own emotion.

Element 2: Cognition Self-reflection and evaluation – know your own values, self-worth, capacities, strengths and weaknesses.

Management of oneself (self-regulation/self-management)
The ability to manage your emotions and motivations, and control them productively.

Element 3: Motivation A positive emotion that drives you towards your goals or aspirations. The ability to perform consistently in a range of situations under pressure. The ability to maintain commitment and take a course of action to achieve your objectives in the face of obstacles, personal challenges or criticism. The ability to manage your awareness of emotion and control it productively. For example, resilience measures whether you are able to pick yourself up and bounce back when things go badly. Realism measures whether you balance optimism with realism.

Element 4: Control The ability to control disruptive emotions and impulses. It measures whether you are emotionally controlled, namely whether you are free to express your feelings but are in control of whether, how and when you do so.

Element 5: Trustworthiness This also means honesty or integrity. It measures whether you invite the trust of others by being principled, reliable and consistent.

Element 6: Conscientiousness Taking responsibility for personal improvement and performance.

Element 7: Flexibility Measures whether you are able to adapt your thinking and behaviour to match changing situations.

Element 8: Creativity Innovative, comfortable with new ideas and novel applications.

Dimension II: Social competences

These competences reflect how we manage relationships. Social competence is a didactic process as individuals gain insight through social interaction and awareness of others. It consists of the following elements:

- Awareness of others (empathy).
- Management of others (social skills).

Awareness of others (empathy)

Element 9: Understanding (and trust) The ability to see from others' perspectives. Ability to understand the key issues, see the whole picture and draw a clear conclusion when presented with incomplete or ambiguous information. It measures whether you trust others but also protect yourself from exploitation.

Element 10: Empowering Help develop others to satisfy their needs and achieve their aspirations.

Management of others (social skills)
The ability to influence, collaborate and cooperate with others by identifying a common ground, shared objectives, taking a leadership role, managing team spirit, resolving any conflicts and communicating clearly with a display of interpersonal sensitivity.

Element 11: Communication Listening to others' points of view. Provide clear and convincing messages about your position and rationale.

Element 12: Facilitating conflict resolution Measure how well you can balance the requirements to be assertive (standing up for what you want) but staying calm and respecting others whilst you are doing it. Help mentees/coachees handle conflict. The coaches and mentors engage the emotional and social aspects when confronting conflicts.

Element 13: Leadership facilitation inspiring Providing guidance to individuals and groups.

Element 14: Coaching the team Creating synergy in team or group coaching to achieve collective objectives.

Element 15: Coaching for change Championing change and modernization.

Dimension III: Cultural competences

These competences reflect how we manage organizational change. It includes the organizational environment (from awareness, appreciation and respect of coachee's/mentee's cultures to help champion the cultural/organizational change).

Cultural competences consist of the following elements:

- Awareness of other cultures (enlightenment).
- Management of organizational cultures (champion).

Cultural competence measures the extent to which coachees inquire into or respond openly to others' cultures, ideas and values; and willingness to challenge and question their own assumptions as well as others'. Coaches and mentors have the ability to mediate boundaries between cultures, connect to others and their own culture. In doing so, we can experience ourselves as part of a larger, collective consciousness, culturally and spiritually. We can recognize that collective awareness and morality transform the organization and society as a whole.

Awareness of other cultures (enlightenment)

Element 16: Appreciation Having appreciation of other cultures and religions.

Element 17: Respect Showing respect of the differences in others' cultures.

Management of organizational cultures (champion)

Element 18: Championing equality and diversity Achieving high performance through people from different cultures and backgrounds. To contribute a voice to a collective endeavour.

Dimension IV: Professional competences

This section reviews some coach/mentor knowledge and approaches, which have an impact on coaching/mentoring outcomes. This requires coaches and mentors to adopt professional approaches, giving and seeking authentic feedback to and from others.

The above dimensions and their associated elements may vary according to the type of coachees/mentees and their aspirations that you help to focus on in your engagements. For example, if your coachees/mentees may come from the same culture, working within the same organization, or even the same team as yours (though unlikely by definition of coaching and mentoring), you may be less concerned with the cultural aspects of the interaction, but focus on the aspects of their personal development (self) or social interaction (e.g. developing social skills, emotional intelligence and resilience).

If you have coachees/mentees working from very different cultures and/or organizations, it may require you to pay particular attention to the cultural context that they bring into the coaching space.

The UIF thus offers a highly flexible framework that enables you to apply different coaching skills and techniques within different coaching/mentoring spaces, such as executive coaching (cultural/organizational dimension) and life coaching (self).

A psychometric tool that measures coaching/mentoring competence based on the UIF can be used to provide feedback to coachees/mentees and identify areas for development. Like any psychometric tool, we need to be mindful that the results only provide a 'snapshot' of the coachee's/mentee's condition at the time of responding to the questionnaire. The results may change over time depending on their development. Using it sensibly, it can be a powerful tool for guiding the coaching/mentoring conversation.

The above elements and dimensions are summarized in Tables 6.1 and 6.2.

Table 6.1 Dimensions of the UIF pragmatic model (Law, 2013)

Competence	*I. Personal (Self)*	*II. Social (Other)*	*III. Cultural (Culture)*	*IV. Professional (Competence)*
Awareness	Self-awareness	Empathy	Enlightenment	Reflective practice
Management	Self-regulation	Social skills	Champion	Continuous professional development

Table 6.2 Elements of cross-cultural EI (Law, 2013)

Dimensions	*Elements*	*Qs*
I. Personal competence	1. Emotion	5
	2. Cognition	5
	3. Motivation	5
	4. Control	5
	5. Trustworthiness	5
	6. Conscientiousness	5
	7. Flexibility	5
	8. Creativity	5
II. Social competence	9. Understanding	5
	10. Empowering	5
	11. Communication	5
	12. Facilitating conflict resolution	5
	13. Leadership facilitation	5
	14. Coaching the team	5
	15. Coaching for change	5
III. Cultural competence	16. Appreciation	10
	17. Respect	10
	18. Champion cultural diversity	5
Total		100

The model is consistent with other meta-frameworks (for example, see Petrides and Furnham, 2001; Taylor Marienau and Fiddler, 2000), see Tables 6.3 and 6.4.

The statements provide indicators for respondents to assess their own development intention and thereby improve their future performance. In completing the test, the participants become more aware of how they feel and and their ability to construct knowledge.

Table 6.3 Petrides and Furnham's (2001) 15 components of trait EI (Law, 2014)

Facets	*Perception*
Adaptability	Flexible to adapt to new conditions
Assertiveness	Willing to stand up for one's rights
Emotion expression	Able to communicate one's feeling to others
Emotion management	Able to influence others' feelings
Emotion perception	Clear about one's own and others' feelings
Emotion regulation	Able to control one's emotions
Impulsiveness (low)	Able to hold back one's urges
Relationship skills	Able to have fulfilling personal relationships
Self-esteem	Successful and confident
Self-motivation	Able to drive in the face of adversity
Social competence	Able to network with excellent social skills.
Stress management	Able to regulate stress and withstand pressure
Trait empathy	Able to take others' perspectives
Trait happiness	Cheerful and satisfied with one's life
Trait optimism	Able to 'look on the bright side' of life

Table 6.4 Comparison of the UIF with the development intention model (Law, 2014)

UIF	*Development intention model*
Personal competence (self-awareness)	Toward knowing as dialogical process
Personal competence (self-awareness: cognition)	Toward a dialogical relationship to oneself
Professional competence	Toward being a continuous learner
Personal competence (self-management)	Toward self-agency and self-authorship
Social/cultural competence	Toward connection with others

Exercise 6.6

So far, you have learnt two models of coaching: the GROW model and the Universal Integrative Framework (UIF). Can you compare and contrast the similarities and differences between the two?

____

____

____

____

The similarities and differences between the two models in terms of their epistemology, development and practices are summarized in Table 6.5.

Table 6.5 Comparison of the UIF with the GROW model

Scope	*Elements*	*GROW*	*UIF*
Epistemology	Grounded in experiences	✓	✓
	Foundation	?	Positive psychology and learning
	Theory	X	✓ Learning theory
Research	Evidence based	?	✓
System	Elements	✓ Goal Reality Option Will	✓ Personal Social Cultural Professional
Process		✓ Linear	X
Structure		✓ Linear; cyclical	✓ Spatial
Emphasis		Goal	Culture
Applications	Leadership, executive coaching	✓	✓
	Life coaching	✓	✓
Characteristics	Continuous professional development and supervision	X	✓
	Coach/Mentor/Client fluidity/integrative continuum	✓	✓
	Cultural Social Competence online self-assessment questionnaire and feedback mechanisms	*X*	✓

Exercise 6.7

How would you apply each model or a combination of the two as an integrative model in your own coaching or mentoring practice?

____

____

____

____

UIF Revisited

From my experience of teaching the UIF and coaching over the years, I have noted the following critiques and feedback:

1. While the UIF criticizes the European frameworks as Euro-centric, the model shows the notion of the self at its centre. Isn't the model itself self-centred and also Euro-centric?
2. The four dimensions can be arranged into different forms and shapes as the relationship between them may vary from culture to culture.
3. It is not easy to apply the framework in practice in comparison with other linear models, such as the GROW model.

Law (2014) shows a number of alternative models of the UIF from various workshops and here three more are added for your interest (see Figures 6.3–6.5).

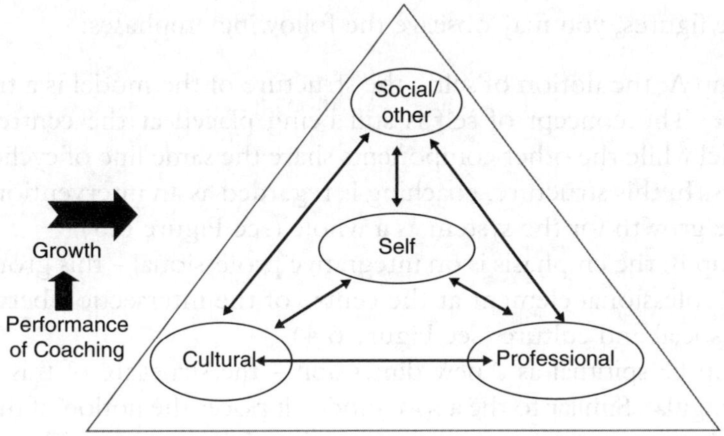

Figure 6.3 The Universal Integrated Framework - Reconfiguration (Group A)

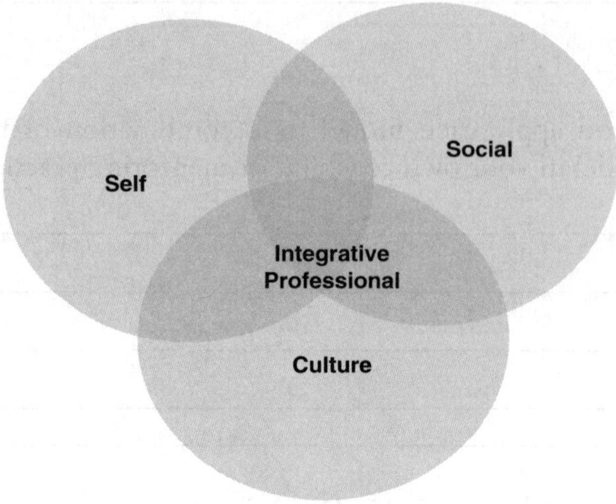

Figure 6.4 The Universal Integrated Framework - Reconfiguration (Group B)

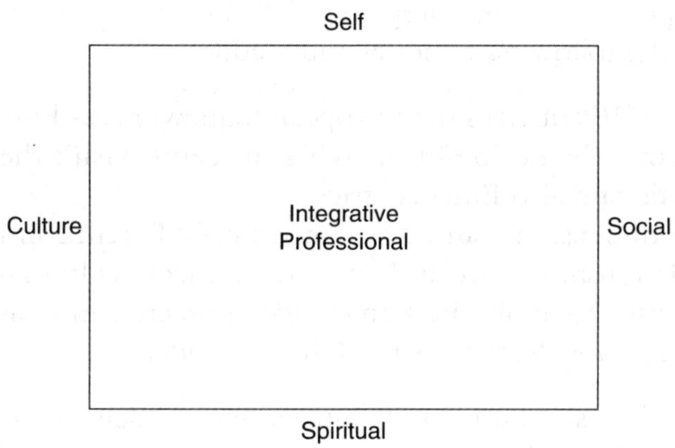

Figure 6.5 The Universal Integrated Framework - Reconfiguration (Group C)

From the figures, you may observe the following emphases:

1. Group A: the notion of self – the structure of the model is a triangular shape. The concept of self is still being placed at the centre of the model while the other components share the same line of cyclical influences. In this structure, coaching is regarded as an intervention to promote growth for the system as a whole (see Figure 6.3).
2. Group B: the emphasis is on integrative professional – this group places the professional element at the centre of the intersection between the self, social and culture (see Figure 6.4).
3. Group C: spiritual as a new dimension – the structure of this model is rectangular. Similar to the above model, it places the notion of the professional element at the centre of intersection. It regards other dimensions as equal entities that surround (box-in) the professional area (see Figure 6.5).

Exercise 6.8

Look at Figures 6.3–6.5. What do you observe? Make a note in terms of the position of each component (self, social, cultural and professional).

What does each new arrangement represent?

What does it signify?

What does it emphasize?

____

____

____

____

Based on the concept of learning culture (discussed in Chapter 3) and using a systems approach, a new system called the Integrative Learning System (ILS) is proposed (see Figure 6.6). This effectively provides a systems map showing both the structure and the inter-relationship between each subsystem and/or component (their boundaries, and so on).

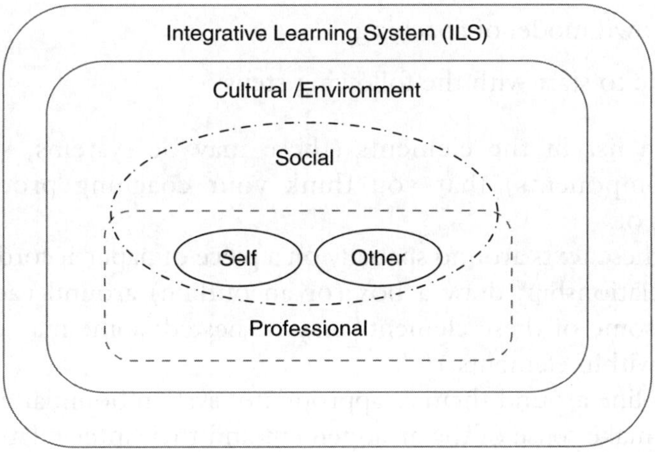

Figure 6.6 The Revised UIF – an Integrative Learning System. Source: Law, 2013

Exercise 6.9

Look at Figure 6.6 and try to make sense of the diagram.

What does this system (ILS) consist of?

What are the components within the social system?

What are the components within the professional system?

Why are some of the boundaries represented by broken lines and others by solid lines?

____

____

____

____

Building Your Own Model of Coaching

I hope by now you understand that you are free to build your own coaching model. Why not have a go?

Exercise 6.10

Draw your own model of coaching.

You may like to start with the following steps:

1. Make a list of the elements (these may be systems, sub-systems and components) that you think your coaching process should consist of.
2. Move these texts around spatially on a piece of paper according to their inter-relationship; draw a box (or an outline) around each element. (Note some of these elements may be nested; some may contain elements within elements.)
3. Draw a line around them as appropriate (system boundaries).
4. Try to make sense of the arrangement and their inter-relationship.

5. Finally, give it a name. What do you call your model of coaching?

____

____

____

____

So now you have your own model of coaching. How would you apply it in your practice? Write a coaching procedure (step-by-step guide) on how you would apply such a model in your coaching session.

____

____

____

____

Chapter Summary and Reflection

In this chapter, you have learnt about two very different models of coaching – GROW and UIF. While UIF/ILS may be regarded as a spatial model with the emphasis on the fluidity and leverage of the cultural environment in relation to other dimensions (self and social interactions), and how all these dimensions may be integrated into the professional dimension; the GROW model is relatively simple and easy to use as it provides a relatively linear step-by-step procedure for coaching. However, coaches are advised not to follow the model rigidly.

You have also been shown how a model such as UIF may be reconfigured in terms of its structure and elements. We have examined four dimensions of competences in coaching that you would need to develop as a coach who aspires to work across cultures. I hope that you can use these frameworks and processes as the basis on which to build your own model of coaching.

In the next two chapters you will learn more about the techniques in relation to UIF/ILS, and undertake some practical exercises, so that hopefully, through practice, you will make your coaching a seamless process.

7

Techniques and Tools

What is in your tool box?

Introduction

This chapter provides you with a set of tools and techniques that will help you to:

- Structure your coaching process.
- Encourage your coachees to formulate their goals and identify the areas of development.
- Identify challenges in the process.
- Continue to refine your own coaching model.
- Conduct coaching conversations (in one-to-one and/or group situations).

These are organized around the structure of the UIF/ILS as follows:

1. Self – self-awareness and self-regulation.
2. Social – empathy and social skills.
3. Cultural – enlightenment and champion of cultures.

To integrate the above techniques into your own coaching practice, you need to continue to practise them as part of your continuous professional development (CPD). Chapter 8 offers a number of exercises in relation to the techniques as well as some guidance covering the fourth dimension:

4. Professional – reflective practice and CPD.

Tools for Developing the System of Self

What are the tools and techniques that can help coachees to develop their 'self' dimension?

To answer this question, we need to first identify the components and elements that constitute self as well as the environment that has influences upon them.

Exercise 7.1

In Chapter 6, you learnt about a system approach to building your own model of coaching. Could you use the same procedure to identify the systems and components of the self? (Tips: this may include both psychological and physical components.)

Make a list:

____

____

____

____

And then organize them in a systems diagram.

Your list may include:

- psychological
  - mind
  - emotion – feeling
  - cognition – thinking
  - perception
- physical
  - physiological – sensory perception
  - the brain – neurological pathways and processes
  - behaviours.

If you have drawn a diagram to show their inter-relationship, you will see that indeed all these elements are inter-related or interconnected in such a

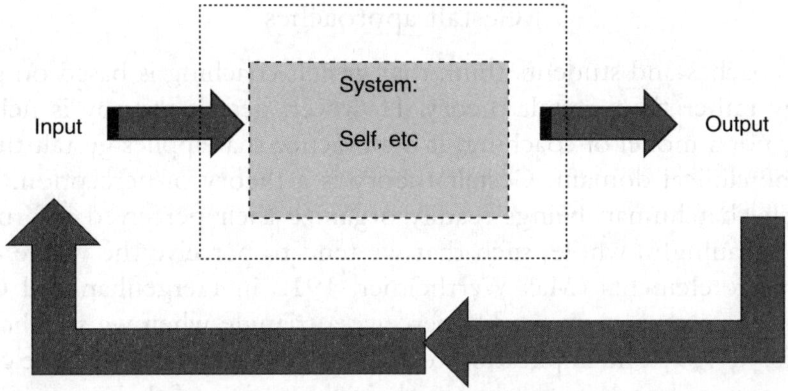

Figure 7.1 A simple system with a feedback loop

way that they influence each other – the sum is greater than the parts. For example, the physical environment (including our or others' behaviour) may have a positive or negative impact upon how we feel. Our emotion may change our thinking, which in turn may influence our behaviour and impact on the environment.

A simple example would be, it is a cold and dull day, and the temperature in the room is making you feel cold. As you become aware of the feeling, you think, 'I need to turn up the thermostat to increase the temperature in the room'. So you actually take action to turn up the thermostat which would change the environment and your feeling too. In systems terms, this is a simple feedback system, which is characteristic of most nature systems. See Figure 7.1.

From this example, you will notice that for an individual, self-awareness is the first step to initiate any change in behaviour.

Tools for Developing Your Self – Awareness and Managing Your Emotion

The tools for developing your self-awareness and managing your emotion outlined in this section include:

- gestalt approaches
- neuro-linguistic programming (NLP)
- cognitive behavioural coaching (CBC).

Gestalt approaches

Many coaches and students think that gestalt coaching is based on gestalt therapy rather than gestalt theory. However, gestalt therapy is neither a theory nor a model of coaching; it is a practice that applies gestalt theories into the clinical domain. Gestalt theory is a theory of perception, which suggests that human beings readily organize their perceived information into a meaningful whole, such that we tend to perceive the whole out of incomplete elements (Max Wertheimer, 1912 in Hergenhan and Olson, 1997). For example, we readily perceive a triangle when we see the three corners: <, V, >. The implication to coaching for change is that the change would require coachees to change their perception of their current situation and to derive new meaning (which I call insightful learning). A good example is to perceive a glass as half full rather than half empty. How do you get coachees to shift their perception from negative to positive? This is a coaching challenge. In this section, I shall describe how you can do that.

The key elements of gestalt coaching are:

- Self-awareness – which is regarded as a starting point for self-regulation and personal growth (Gillie, 2009; Magerman and Leahy, 2009; Perls, 1969, 1973; Simon, 2009).
- Organization (grouping) – we readily organize our perceptual information according to the laws of organization: in terms of the proximity, similarity, closure, simplicity and the 'figure' and 'ground' separation (Koffka, 1935).
- Awareness of others – this focuses on the coaching relationship: the transfer of experiences (from coachees to coaches and vice versa).
- Awareness of the world (the oneness).
- Present – emphasis on the primacy of present-centred attitude, living-in-the-moment.
- Self – as an instrument, thus use self-expressions (verbal, non-verbal, physical gestures) to transform – emphasis on action (including non-action) rather than utterance.
- Compassion – non-judgemental.
- Being – emphases on the experience, emotion and spontaneity rather than knowledge, understanding or intention.

Gestalt psychology and neuro-linguistic programming (NLP)

As the name suggests, one would have thought that NLP should be highly relevant within the realm of psychology – both in theory and in practice. Indeed, NLP has been very popular in the coaching world as well as in many other areas of applications. However, for various reasons, it has not been too popular in the academic and professional worlds of psychology. Owing to its popularity and relevance in relation to the concept of self within the context of coaching, I shall briefly discuss this technique here.

NLP was first developed by John Grinder and Richard Bandler in the 1970s at University of California (Santa Cruz). The first model, called the meta model of therapy (Bandler and Grinder, 1975) was actually developed by modelling the patterns that gestalt therapist Fritz Perls and family therapist Virginia Satir used. The idea was to produce an explicit programme for the therapeutic application. Thus the meta model is effectively a model of gestalt therapy, which was based on the principle of gestalt psychology. In other words, the meta model is more appropriately called the gestalt model.

As we can see from the history of NLP development, there is a clear psychological root that underpins its model of practices. There is ongoing research and development on this topic (Law and Ackland, 2011). Inspired by his former supervisor with this psychological insight, and based on the ideas from Law and Grimley's (2011) initial manuscript coupled with further studies, Bruce Grimley (2012) also explored the psychology of NLP coaching in both theory and practice. Interested readers may wish to follow this up. Here I shall describe the few basic techniques that you may find useful in coaching.

Using the NLP meta model in coaching

The purpose of the meta model in NLP is to challenge the limitations in 'mental maps' (mental representations) carried in the coachee's head, and recover the meaning from the language's deep structure. The meta model can be used in coaching to help coachees to clarify their assumptions, which may be expressed verbally during the coaching conversation. Through responding to a series of questions asked by the coach using the meta model, the coachees become aware of their own assumptions and see new possibilities by expanding and/or revising their own mental maps.

For instance, if the sentences uttered by the coachee were incomplete or vague (regarded by NLP as 'poorly structured'), then the coach can use the meta model of gestalt language pattern to seek clarification. Through the coaching dialogue using the meta model as a framework, the erroneous assumption may be discovered (from the mental representation). These representations may be the source for change if the coachees are to achieve their goals efficiently.

The NLP meta model is a collection of gestalt language patterns. Each pattern consists of the following two steps:

1. Identify a syntactic pattern used by the speaker.
2. Challenge this syntactic pattern so that the speaker's map of possibilities can be expanded (or at least clarified).

The above pattern can be implemented in coaching using the following production rule:

Rule 1: IF the syntactic pattern used by the coachee is ambiguous
THEN Challenge this syntactic pattern.

The above rule can then be applied by the recognize–act cycle procedure as follows:

- Step 1: Apply Rule 1.
- Step 2: Repeat Rule 1 until it fails (i.e. no more ambiguity, the condition has been clarified).

Let's illustrate how the above works with the following example:

'*Teaching is boring*'

Think about it. The surface structure of the above statement is actually quite ambiguous. We may interpret it in at least two different ways (maybe more), with two deep structures:

'***What is being taught is boring***'

Or

'*It is boring for X to teach*'

where X is a person, who may be me, you, him, her or them.

Either of the above interpretations could be the one that the coachee is referring to.

Another advantage of using the meta model is that it often recovers what has been deleted in the surface structure. For instance in the alternative deep structures above, we still do not know how the teaching was done, when and under what conditions it was boring, and so on. Further questioning using the meta model would clarify the meaning of the sentence.

From modelling Fritz Perls' and Virginia Satir's gestalt practice, Richard Bandler and John Grinder identified the following patterns that were common to their approach:

- Noun challenge – Who?
- Verb challenge – How?
- Universal quantifier challenge.
- Mind-reading challenge – How do you know what others think?
- Cause–effect semantic ill-formedness challenge – How specifically?
- Complex equivalence challenge – Does 'IF x THEN y' mean 'x = y'?

John Grinder used his knowledge in the transformational grammar (Chomsky, 1965) and identified more syntax that was found to be useful. As a result, a number of syntactic patterns were identified in the meta model. These syntactic patterns reveal how our represented world (external map) is misrepresented in our representing world (internal map). These syntactic patterns can be grouped into three general categories in terms of their underlying misrepresentation:

- deletion
- distortion
- generalization.

Deletion

Deletion is when bits of components in our represented world have gone missing through an initial perceptual stage – Grinder called this the first access (Bostic St. Clair and Grinder (2001) and the subsequent recognition (second access), which I denote these stages as f^1 and f^2 processes respectively. For instance, in conversation, some of the information was spoken but not heard. This may not be due to the fact that the voice was too quiet or the person could not hear, but because the information was deleted in the process of perception.

Distortion

Distortion is the phenomenon when the represented world is distorted in our representing world. For instance, have you ever noticed that sometimes, when you say something to a person, the listeners completely mishear what you have said or interpret it differently? People with a spider phobia may see spiders much bigger than they really are. Those who suffer from anorexia nervosa may see their body size much larger than their actual figure. In both cases, the represented world has been distorted.

Generalization

Generalization is the situation when a conclusion is drawn with limited information. This is due to the fact that generalization requires less memory (the 'cognitive economy' principle). Generalization is the root that generates all of the -isms in our perception, for example, ageism, racism or sexism. In each case the person holds a typical view about another group of people due to their lack of knowledge about those groups (for example, racial stereotype).

Of course the above categories are arbitrary. Strictly speaking, they all belong to some kind of misrepresentation as a result of our perceptual processes and knowledge representation in our long-term memory. In a coaching situation, if coachees carry an internal map in their mind with a lot of essential elements missing in the represented world, the range of possibilities available to them becomes limited. By using the syntactic patterns of the meta model appropriately in the coaching conversation, the coach can help coachees become aware of their own misrepresentation of the represented world and discover new possibilities. The description of these patterns, with examples of the coachee's statements and the coach's responses, are summarized in Table 7.1.

It may be possible that having applied the meta model to your coachees, they may still continue to misrepresent the represented world. This may be due to the fact that the misrepresentation is stored within their unconscious (a deeper structure), and this also links to their emotion.

Anchoring

This section provides a formal definition of anchoring. It links it to the psychology of learning. Some examples and applications are described.

Anchoring – a common technique used by NLP practitioners – is actually based on a learning theory known as classical conditioning. In his research, Ivan Pavlov (1927) noticed that when presented with food, the dogs salivated. Furthermore, he observed that if a bell rings at the same time when the food is presented to the dogs, over time, the dogs learn to associate the bell (the anchor) with the food. They would salivate even if only the bell is ringing. Pavlov's classical conditioning consists of the following stages:

1. Unconditioned Stimulus (US) => Unconditioned Response (UR)

   e.g. Food => Salivation

2. US + Conditioned Stimulus (CS) => UR

   e.g. Food + Bell => Salivation

Table 7.1 Syntactic patterns in the meta model

Language pattern	*Description*	*Example of coachee's statement*	*Example of coach's response*
Deletions:			
Simple deletion	Information is missing	They do …	*Do what?*
Unspecified comparatives	To whom or what is it being compared? '*…than what or whom?*'	I performed better yesterday	*Compared with whom?*
Unspecified verb	How is not specified '*How specifically?*'	She taught herself…	*How did she teach herself?*
Lack of referential index	Does not specify to whom it refers	They learn it quickly	*Who learns?* *Who specifically?*
Lost performative	Value judgement – by whom? '*Who says?*'	It's wrong to bad mouth people	*Who says so? How do you know it is wrong?*
Distortions:			
Nominalization	When verbs turned into nouns	His performance is poor	*How could he perform better?*
Cause and effect	Implying one thing causes another, but the actual causal mechanism was not specified x causes y to happen. '*How does x cause y?*'	You irritate me	*How specifically do I irritate you?*
Presupposition	Making assumptions or presupposition, which has been taken for granted	When you are educated you will understand this	*What leads you to believe … ?* *How specifically will … ?*

(Continued)

Table 7.1 *(Cont'd)*

Language pattern	*Description*	*Example of coachee's statement*	*Example of coach's response*
Mind reading	Claiming to know someone's thoughts	David is miserable	*How do you know? What leads you to believe that?*
Complex equivalence	Implying two things are equal. X $\Leftrightarrow$ Y	You never listen to me (…pause…) You never provide eye contact	*So not providing eye contact means I am not listening to you?* *How does x mean y?*
Generalizations:			
Universal quantifiers	All, every, etc.	All NLP courses are too expensive	*ALL NLP courses are too expensive? Which one specifically? Are there any exceptions to that?*
Modal operator of possibility	Might, could, etc.	I can't get myself organized	*What would happen if you did? What prevents you? What would happen if you could?*
Modal operator of necessity	Must, should, etc.	I shouldn't interrupt when people are talking	*What would happen if you did? What stops you?*

3. CS => Conditioned Response or learned response (CR)

e.g. Bell => Salivation

Thus, anchoring is an internal response that may be triggered by external or internal stimuli. Anchoring is the process by which we necessarily make associations between the memory of our experiences (long-term memory) and our sensory experiences (mental representation). Bostic St. Clair and Grinder (2001: 199) define anchoring as 'a set of operations for bundling and manipulating otherwise undifferentiated groupings' within the mental representation of our senses (which they call 5-tuples) with the intention of bringing them into contact with other mental representations for purposes of differentiation or integration.

In the NLP context, the 5-tuple represents our five sensory registers:

- **V**isual – seeing (V^i)
- **A**uditory – hearing (A^d)
- **K**inaesthetic – feeling (K^i)
- **G**ustatory – tasting (G^u)
- **O**lfactory – smelling (O^l)

Our sensory registers may associate with different kinds of experiences that we have had in the past (via a process of classical conditioning). These associations can be useful for our everyday response to the environment, for example red traffic light and stopping. They can be pleasurable, for instance the smell of cut grass and childhood summers; or unpleasant, for example the sound of a police car siren and feeling apprehensive. The connections we form between combinations of sights, sounds, feelings, smells and tastes determine our responses to different situations. These naturally occurring anchors are formed in the course of our own personal history. Think of meeting someone and getting that internal feeling instantly each time you see or hear them. That is anchoring.

Anchors are useful and adaptive when we find ourselves responding spontaneously in ways that work for us, for example feeling calm and resourceful in the face of danger. On the other hand, when we find ourselves responding in ways which are not useful to us, for example feeling inadequate at interviews, we have simply made an inappropriate association between the two – internal experiences (e.g. feeling inadequate) and the external situation (e.g. being in an interview). The association between our behavioural response (R) and the external stimulus (S) forms a pattern of connections over time (a process known as classical conditioning within the domain of S–R [Stimulus–Response] psychology). S is also referred to as a 'trigger' in NLP. The extreme case of a negative or maladaptive anchor is a phobia or post-traumatic stress disorder (PTSD), where choice is severely limited by a compelling connection between the S–R pair (e.g. see S = spider; R = feel terrified). Very often, S–R associations are misinterpreted as similar to production rules, for instance:

IF <condition: S = spider> THEN <action: R = feel terrified>

Such an analogy is erroneous. Since the S–R pair directly links to a neuro-pathway, it is an automatic process. In other words, one cannot help but feel terrified in the face of danger (such as seeing a spider, or attending an interview) – a reactive response. There are no IF–THEN decision-making cognitive processes. Both are forms of learning. One is passive; and the other is active. The S–R process is unconscious; decision making is conscious at least at the early stage of the process. Although condition rules can become automatic (unconscious), they usually require a lot of practice, which is a characteristic of the expert's behaviour.

Also, it is important to note that although S stimulus is usually thought to be external, this is not always necessary. For instance, once the S–R pattern (anchor) is established, an imagination or visualization (internal stimulus) may be enough to trigger the S–R response.

One of the contributions of behavioural psychology (especially classical conditioning) to NLP is the manipulation of anchors. This is based on our understanding of the fact that the first perception (R^1) and Post-R^1 representation (R^2) are two different things. Thus, when facing negative anchors (S–R pairs) we can simply disconnect R^2 from R^1 (dissociation). Furthermore, we can choose to replace R^2 with a new form of representation, say R^{2N} that is more desirable. For example, in the past, a person may have been conditioned to feel inadequate at interviews. Using NLP anchoring techniques, that person can be re-conditioned to feel confident and energetic in interviews if that is what is preferred. We shall describe these anchoring techniques next.

Anchoring – how it works in practice

From the above section, we can see that anchoring may be used in coaching and many other forms of 'change work' (such as treating phobias and PTSD). Whatever the condition, say in coaching, personal development or organizational change, typically we have the following set of S–R patterns (negative and positive anchors):

Current situation (undesirable): negative anchor = S_0–R_0
Goal (positive state, desirable): positive anchor = S_1–R_1

where S_0 is the original negative stimulus; R_0 the original negative state/response; S_1 a new positive stimulus and R_1 a new positive state/response.

Throughout this book, we have repeatedly emphasized that NLP is all about manipulation of representations. Here (S_0–R_0) and (S_1–R_1) are two sets of representations. Thus in NLP terms, all we need to do is manipulate all the variables: S_0, S_1, R_0 and R_1 within these two sets and thereby replace R_0 with R_1 by pairing (S_0–S_1) together. The key variable in this manipulation is S_1 which in NLP we call an 'anchor'. An anchor is the key stimulus that can trigger a set of experiences (positive or negative). We shall explain how the process works in detail. In general (i cases), this takes the following steps:

1. Elicit physiological states (R_i).
2. Calibrate R_i.
3. Set anchors (S_i).

We will discuss these steps in turn and then show how they can be applied to more specific contexts with some examples.

Step 1: Elicit physiological states (R_i). Your physiological state is more than just how you feel. It is the sum total of all the physiological and neurological processes within you at any moment in time. The state you are in has a profound impact on your capabilities and your interpretation of experience. The more fully you re-experience a memory, the more likely you are to re-access the physiological state you were in at the time the memory was formed and vice versa (this is called episodic memory or 'state-dependent memory' in NLP, and it is an analogical representation). In eliciting your own states you usually make full use of all your sensory representations (FA). In eliciting states in others you can elicit these representations by asking:

> Go back there in imagination and become aware of where you are and what you are seeing. As you are back there, listen to the sounds. Put your body into the same position and let the sensations and feelings intensify.

To help lead your coachees into the desired state, it will help if you make your behaviour congruent with theirs by going into the state yourself.

When eliciting physiological states, two aspects are critical. One is the *intensity* of the state: when you anchor it, and later fire the anchor, you will usually get a weaker state. The other is the *purity* of the state: ensure that the experience chosen is a clean example of the desired state, and is not contaminated with a different state.

Step 2: Calibrate R_i. As your coachees re-access their previous experience, use full sensory acuity to detect the external cues of their internal state.

These cues may be obvious or minimal (e.g. small changes in facial muscle tone, breathing rhythm, skin colour or pupil dilation). These external cues let you know when the experience is at peak intensity. If you are self-anchoring, calibrate directly to the internal cues of your own states, for instance from 'stuck' states to 'excellence' states. Increasing awareness of your own internal states will increase your effectiveness at monitoring your own performance. You will find yourself spending less and less time in the 'stuck' state, and more and more time in the state of excellence.

Set anchors (S_i). You can anchor a state with any sensory stimuli in any combination: ***visually*** with a gesture or expression; ***auditory*** with a key word or voice tone; and ***kinaesthetically*** with a touch. Whatever anchors you use, it is critical that they are distinctive and unique to prevent contamination with other associations. The timing is also critical. Anchor just before the experience comes up to peak intensity. Any later, and your anchor will go out of the experience. Finally, you must be able to reproduce the anchor accurately and precisely. If you do not, you will get only a partial access of the state. When you have established an anchor, immediately break the state by redirecting your attention elsewhere. Then test the anchor by 'firing' it again. If you do not see the external physiological cues that let you know the internal state has been accessed, repeat the anchoring process, paying particular attention to the six critical elements of effective anchoring:

- *Intensity* of physiological state.
- *Purity* of physiological state.
- *Calibration* to external cues of the internal state.
- *Uniqueness* of the anchor.
- *Timing* the anchor just before peak state.
- *Accuracy* in duplicating anchor.

For further examples of using anchoring in NLP, see O'Connor and Lages (2004).

The paradoxical theory of change

Gestalt theory suggests that change is a natural and continuous process, called the gestalt cycle of continuous flow of experience (Beisser, 1970; Melnick and Nevis, 2005). Figure 7.2 shows the relationship between our energy expenditure for activities and the associated awareness of that experience. Initially we are unaware of the world out there (the default state, arbitrarily denoted as –1 in the figure). Sometimes, we may

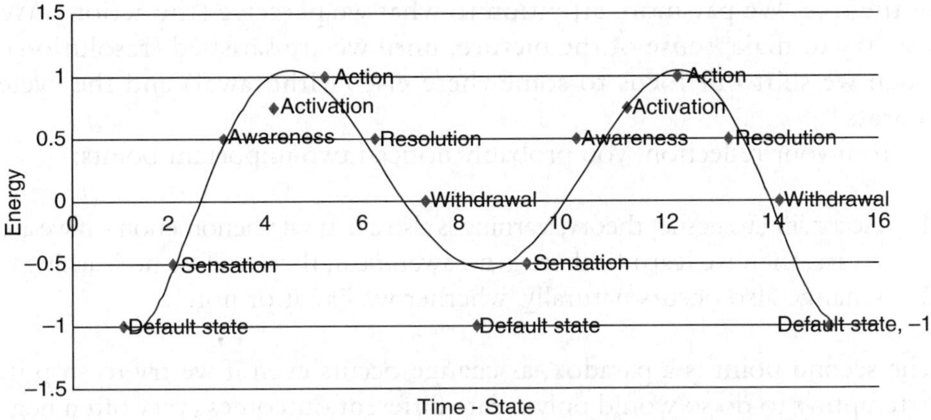

Figure 7.2 A conceptual plot for the gestalt cycle of continuous flow of experience

Technical note: the chart uses the polynomial plot to show the relationship between the energy expenditure (arbitrary value) and event sequence (time-state). 0 to +1 represents the realm of conscious awareness; 0 to −1: internal sensation (unconscious).

sense something but are still not fully aware of it; gradually we become aware of this something, say, it is an abstract painting on the wall, a tree outside the window. This forms a 'figure of interest'. It activates our energy to respond to it. For instance, we may appreciate the beauty of the painting in the room or the change of colour in the autumn leaves

Exercise 7.2

Compare the gestalt cycle of continuous flow of experience and the learning cycle. What are the similarities and differences?

Map the stages of the gestalt cycle onto the learning cycle.

What are the implications of the gestalt cycle to learning, and our ability to initiate change?

of the tree. We pay more attention to what we perceive (the action). We may try to make sense of the picture, until we are satisfied (resolution). Then we shift our focus to somewhere else (withdrawal) and the cycle repeats.

From your reflection, you probably noticed two important points:

1. According to gestalt theory, learning is also a natural phenomenon – if we are aware, then we learn (if there is no awareness, there will be no learning).
2. Change also occurs naturally, whether we like it or not.

The second point is a paradox, as change occurs even if we try to stop it. Attempting to do so would only create different outcomes (very often negative ones). Therefore, accept what happens; it is what it is; then direct your energy to deal with it accordingly.

More importantly, change always occurs in the here-and-now, moment by moment. So if we want to take responsibility for the change that is taking place, we need to pay attention to our present moment.

Exercise 7.3

What are the implications of the paradox of change to coaching? (Hint: think what would happen to your coachees who were in denial or in resistance of the change that is happening in their life.)

How would you apply this theory into your coaching practice?

What would you do if you noticed that your coachee showed signs of resistance during a coaching session?

____

____

____

____

Tackling resistance

Applying the paradoxical theory of change to coaching may help the coachee to simply focus on the present moment (such as mindfulness exercises described in the next chapter). Surprisingly, a new insight may emerge. Choosing to ask a question that challenges a coachee's resistance, a typical coaching question often practised by NLP practitioner – What stops you? – is an example of modelling the gestalt approach on tackling resistance (the meta model). However, for such a question to work, the coach needs to first direct the coachees to focus on the here-and-now, and examine what really is stopping them from achieving their goal.

Gestalt techniques

Gestalt techniques include:

- Suppression – suppress resistance. Try to do nothing, to experience nothing. Try it; you will find that it is extremely hard, almost impossible! This state will provide you with the 'ground' (the default state), within which you become aware – figures of interest emerge. Mindfulness exercises (Chapter 8) will help.

Exercise 7.4

From your reading so far about gestalt techniques (including NLP), what are the do's and don'ts in gestalt coaching?

Make a list:

Do's:

____

____

____

____

Don'ts:

____

____

____

____

- Expression – opposite to suppression. Do something! Express your inner voice. What does it sound like? Draw a picture of your vision. What does it look like? Try to exaggerate the expression. Try to *explicate* the expression by using metaphors or *translate* it into different forms. Act it out as if you were the expression.
- Integration – integrate the past as well as the future 'self' with the 'present self' so they are in one wholeness.

The technique of integration is readily recognized by NLP practitioners in the time-line exercise where coachees are asked to visualize an imaginary line on the floor from where they stand to the points that represent various stages of their future. The coachees are asked to walk along that imaginary line and learn from that experience, and bring those resources and skills back into the present.

The techniques can be applied to integrate other personalities within a person to gain an understanding of their character. Again, this is another common approach in NLP modelling.

Managing Your Self – Your Cognition and Emotion – Cognitive Behavioural Coaching (CBC)

Aaron Beck *et al.* (1979) developed cognitive behaviour therapy (CBT). This has rapidly become a popular intervention within the health sector (Chambless, 1988; Rothbaum *et al.*, 2000). For a useful reference manual, see Greenberger and Padesky (1995). CBT has very often been used in coaching, and some practitioners refer to the technique as cognitive behavioural coaching (CBC; also see Law, 2014; Neenan and Palmer, 2001; Palmer and Whybrow, 2004).

CBC makes use of Socratic dialogue to challenge the coachee's assumptions (schema) and cognitions which are often used in coaching (Allan and Law, 2009; Szymanska, 2008). In doing so, it helps coachees to change their way of thinking and thereby their emotion and behaviour. The CBC approach consists of the following steps:

1. Examine the current and/or recent past situation – assess current emotion and cognition. Questions include: How do/did you feel? What were you thinking about in association with those feelings?
2. Set a goal – get the coachee to assign a value to the goal. For example, on a scale of 1–10 how committed are you to achieve the goal? Or if the coachee prefers, on a scale of 1–100% (it is arbitrary).

3. Set SMARTER objectives – break the goal down into SMARTER objectives (see Chapter 6).
4. Assess the emotion of coachees – link those objectives with the coachee's emotion. For example, how do you feel about achieving this objective by next week? A similar scale can also be used to measure the intensity of the coachee's feelings.
5. Identify possible barriers that may hinder the progress in achieving those objectives, including physical, social and psychological aspects (cognitive barriers) such as performance interfering thinking (PIT; Neenan and Palmer, 2001).
6. Develop strategies to overcome barriers – help the coachee to develop performance enhancing thinking (PET; Neenan and Palmer, 2001), and an action plan to overcome the identified barriers.
7. Review progress, as part of the evaluation and review process, providing the coachee with feedback.

The seven steps are summarized in Figure 7.3.

In practice, if you monitor your coachees' emotions each session, you will see that they go up and down (see Figure 7.4).

However, over a period of time, if CBT does work, their positive emotion should move in the right direction; that is the positive emotion should go up and maintain a high level; while the negative emotion should go down or disappear altogether. See Figure 7.5.

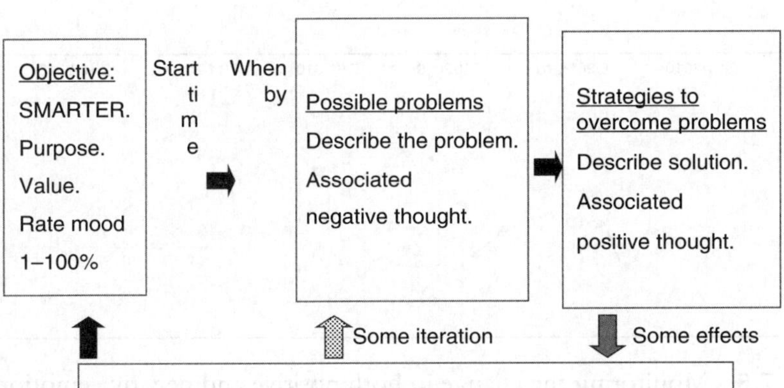

Figure 7.3 Schematic diagram showing the process of CBC.

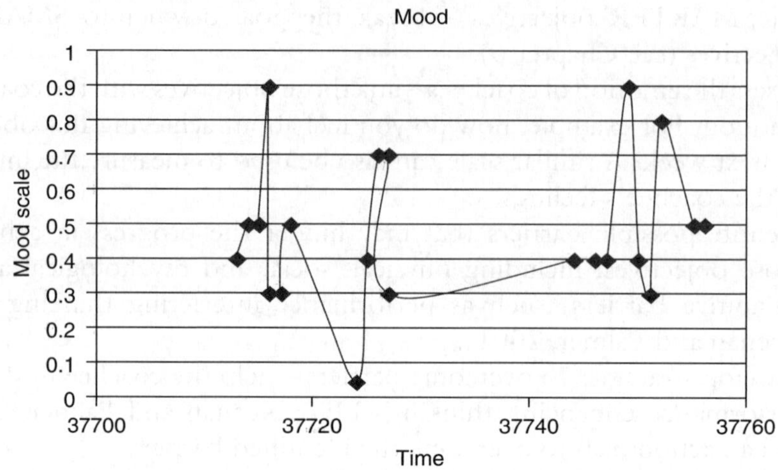

Figure 7.4 Monitoring the change in emotion over time showing the variation of the coachee's emotion (the time is arbitrary for demonstration only)

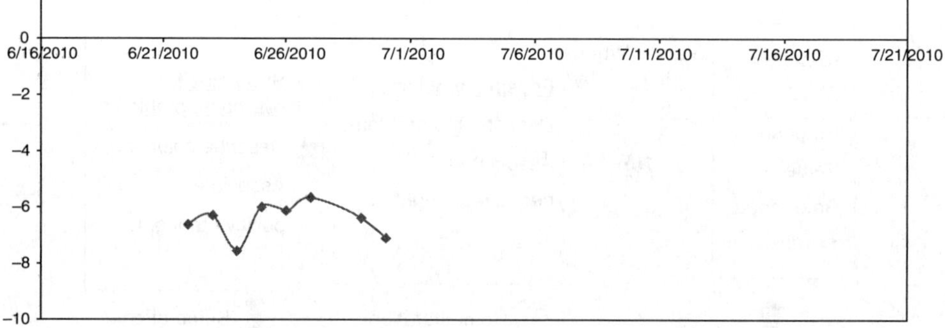

Figure 7.5 Monitoring the change in both positive and negative emotions over time showing that the coachee's negative emotion went down and disappeared altogether and was replaced by the presence of the positive emotion; and the positive emotion continuously increased (the dates are fictitious for demonstration only)

Key: Black line – positive emotion. Grey line – negative emotion

Exercise 7.5

Table 7.2 shows a list of emotions reported by a client before and after a CBT programme. Can you see the impact of the CBT upon this particular client?

Table 7.2 A mood table showing the change of emotion before and after a CBT intervention

Before	*After*
Anxious, restless, impatient	N/A
Worried, anxious, apprehensive, guilty	N/A
Stressed, frustrated	N/A
Embarrassed, stupid, angry	N/A
Guilty, frustrated	N/A
Selfish	N/A
Undecided, sad, guilty	N/A
Frustrated, angry, fed up	N/A
Worried, helpless, apprehensive, concerned	Laugh at oneself – feeling previously one was stupid, silly, frustrated, ridiculous
N/A	Happy, proud
N/A	Enlightened

How would you evaluate this impact quantitatively?

Just like the example presented in Figure 7.5, you can ask your clients to report their emotions on a Likert scale (say, 1–10), then you may monitor and evaluate the change quantitatively.

The Social Context in Coaching or Mentoring – The Self and Others

Existential coaching

Existentialism is neither theory nor model; it is a philosophy. It was developed by Søren Kierkegaard who proposed that each individual is responsible for constructing meaning to their own life (being true to oneself). Existentialism became popular in the years after the Second World War when many individuals reflected on their own mortality and meaning, having experienced the trauma of the war. Existentialism starts with a set of assumptions about the universal human condition:

- Isolation – we were all born alone and will go alone.
- Death is certain but the condition (how and when) is uncertain.
- Meaninglessness – the above thoughts lead us to question the meaning and purpose of life.

This causes anxiety – so-called existential angst. To apply the existential philosophical approach to coaching, we need to develop a model of existential coaching from the existential philosophy. I shall describe this model next.

The ABC existential model of coaching

The key elements of existential coaching are based on the following existential concerns:

A. Awareness – aware of our being, aware that we are finite – experience of time.
B. Being meaningful – meaningfulness.
C. Choice – we can choose, therefore we exist, as a free agent. Courage to confront, to choose, that is what makes human behaviour unpredictable.

Awareness of time

Unlike gestalt approaches, within the existential context, being aware of time means being one's own time; being ... aware of the flow of time ... past–present–future ... in the process of becoming .... There is a certain quality about one's own time – its open-endedness, progression, circumscribed nature, irrevocability and finiteness.
Your list of factors may include:

- activity
- context
- culture
- mood
- society
- stages of life – significant moments, events, milestones.

Exercise 7.6

What are the triggers to such emotion and thoughts?

Make three lists (A, B and C) of items that provide you with a sense of past, present and future, respectively (e.g. past: photographs, paintings)

Now reflect upon the above items. Make a list of factors that you think influence your experience of time. Have you experienced any difficulties in doing this, especially List C? Some cultures do not have a concept of 'future' (Mbiti, 1969).

Implications to coaching In his workshop at the BPS SGCP Conference on 19 December 2005, Professor Ernesto Spinelli criticized the present-/future-focused approach of coaching from the existential perspective of time on two grounds:

1. Over-reliance on the present – no continuity; empty self – just of the moment, no substance; no lasting purpose, contribution or meaning.
2. Over-reliance on the future – paradoxically, eradicates the future and always leaves one's experience of the present as 'something to come'. I keep jumping from one empty future possibility that is 'now' to the next and the next – never connecting, never stopping to examine or to see the worth of examination.

Being meaningful – existential meaning

Existentialism assumes that we are meaning-making beings. We interpret the world via our neurophysiological process (compare to NLP). We have an intentionality to search for meaning. It is our intentionality to interpret the world and make meaning. As individuals are different, each one's own meaning is different. There is no single (truth) version of meaning; it is neither fixed nor absolute. Owing to the uncertainty of the human condition, how we make meaning is also uncertain – it is fluid. Such meaning-making is inter-rational. Meaning is constructed in relation to the other. It cannot be considered in isolation but can only be understood in the inter-relational context. Meaning is co-created by self–other; self/subject–object (Heidegger, 1962). There are different kinds of meanings, for example:

- actualization – (Maslow, 1954)
- altruism – serving others
- creativity
- dedication to a cause
- hedonism – pleasure principle
- experience of beauty
- fortitude – the capacity to face up to adversity and find meaning in doing so (used in transformational leadership).

Exercise 7.7

The meaning of meaning-making depends on the other.

What does this statement mean?

____

____

____

____

Consider the experience of the existing stance so far; you may be able to sense that conflict is inevitable. It represents the gap between the version of self which one believes one is (perceived self and meaning) and the actual stance/way of being that one adopts (the reality). Conflict arises when we choose not to accept such versions of self or the reality.

Choice – We have to choose!

Despite the finiteness of our existence and the uncertainty of the human condition, we are free to construct our own meaning in relation to others and to the world. Furthermore the existential stance insists that although we may have no control over the situation that has happened to us, we are free to choose our response to it (no matter what and how the situation is) – for 'we are our choices' (Sartre, 1956). Thus autonomy (freedom and free will) and determinism are linked but not opposite. Therefore existentialists take a phenomenological position that, freedom is 'situated' within the given constraint, 'bounded' by a particular time, people, culture and historical context – the so-called 'thrownness' (*Geworfenheit*) (Heidegger, 1962).

Given such a position, individuals have accountability, intentionality and responsibility. We have to choose to embrace anxiety rather than seek to eradicate it. We have to confront it (as an unavoidable 'urgent experience') and be mindful of being rather than ignore or forget about it. This is essential for our authentic existence (authentic self) (Heidegger, 1962).

Look at it another (positive) way: anxiety has its advantages too. It can alert us to the possibility of authentic meaning and 'awaken' us to the opportunity to live a 'good life' (compare with the philosophy of positive psychology). Thus, the solutions to our problems rest upon our individual search for meaning – more meaningful ways to live (being). The above can be summarized in Figure 7.6.

The existential model of coaching shows that at its starting point (A) is our awareness of time, our own mortality, vulnerability and the uncertainty which cause anxiety (existential angst). The solution that the existential

Exercise 7.8

What if we deny our own freedom to choose?

What would be the consequences?
– To the person?
– To the way they interact with others?

____

____

____

____

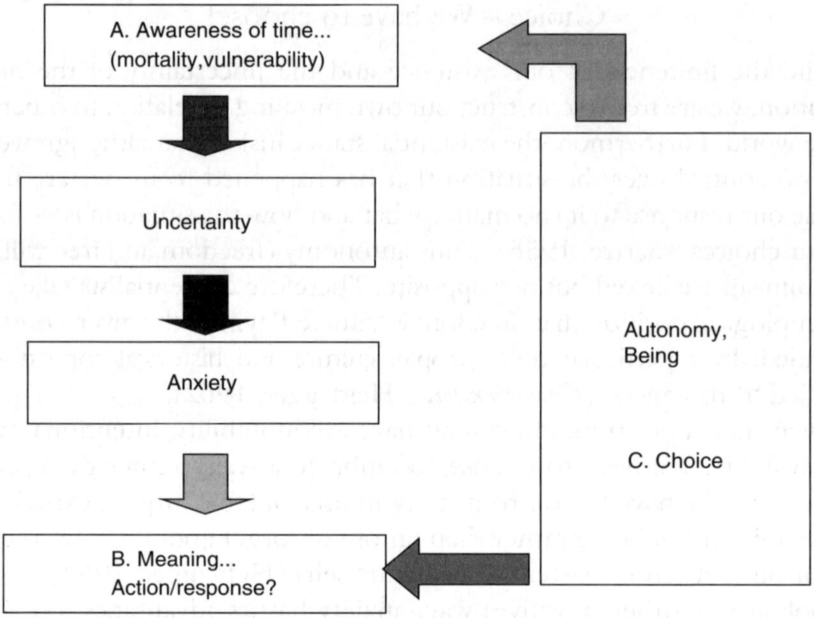

Figure 7.6 The ABC existential model of coaching

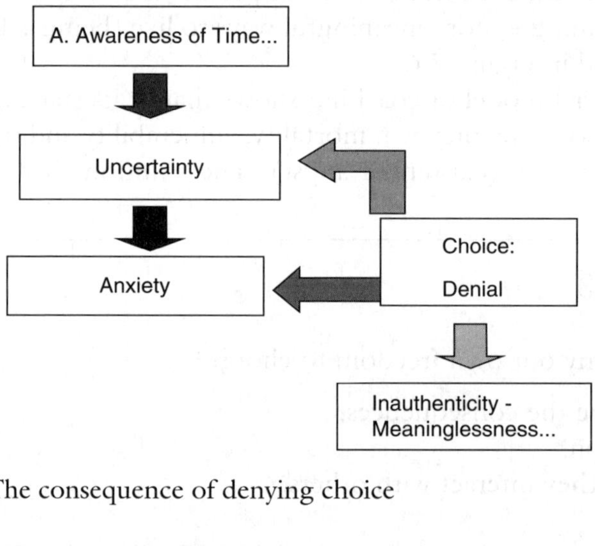

Figure 7.7 The consequence of denying choice

approach offers is that we need to understand that we have autonomy to choose and construct our own meaning out of such a situation.

If we refuse to come to terms with such a human condition and are not able to recognize that we have responsibility to choose, we will only continue to suffer existential angst and live inauthentic lives with meaninglessness as a result. See Figure 7.7.

Applying the existential model to coaching

As a phenomenological approach, existential coaching uses the following phenomenological rules:

1. The rule of epoche – no presupposition, value objectivity (bracket assumptions, bias).
2. The rule of description – what and how (e.g. tell a story – describe don't explain).
3. The rule of horizontalization – value equality (don't place hierarchies of significance).

Take the existential notion (the discourse on the inter-relational realm) that we are always in relation to:

1. Self: I-focus – about myself.
2. Others: You-focus – about you; or they-focus – about them.
3. Our world: We-focus – about us.

Existential coaching aims to address the existential angst by applying the above three rules to coaching and the coaching relationship (see Spinelli and Horner, 2007). I shall describe these in turn.

Relationship with self

Existential coaching focuses on one's lived experience and its meaning (meaningful experience). Thus in existential coaching, setting goals or planning change may not be its prime objective. Coaching questions may include:

- What is it like to be …?
- What does it (this experience) mean to you?

Existential coaching pays equal focus to the divided stances, aims and aspirations that may exist as competing values and beliefs held by each coachee.

Existential coaching focuses on meaningful relationships. It aims to help coachees to clarify and reconsider meanings they have given to their relationships and how their stance impacts on the quality and enjoyment of their own lives as well as those of others.

Existential coaching focuses on the inter-relational context, on the coachee's relationship with his/her self. For example, the coach may ask:

- What would you tell yourself about being you (who you are) in this (any) relationship?

Relationship with others (the inter-relational realms) – being with others?
For the existential coach, the success of coaching depends on the development of a trustworthy coaching relationship. First of all, an existential coach focuses on the coaching relationship (the coachee and I) – the coachee's experience of 'us' which represents the relationship with the coach. Secondly, the coach focuses on the coachee's experience of others. For example, the coach may ask:

- What do you tell yourself about the other's experience of being with you in this (any given) encounter?

Relationship with the world – me in the world?
Existential coaching focuses on the coachee's worldview. It emphasizes on their way of being in the world, not on just doing. It relies on the coach's and coachee's experience of being in relation with one another, which reflects the whole of their worldview. The coach may invite the coachee to consider the following questions:

- What do I tell myself about the meaning?
- What impact would my new stance have on significant others?

Existential coaching applications

The existential approach may be very useful for coachees who are in transition (such as changing job or entering a new relationship). It would help coachees to:

- Increase understanding of their individual stance to life.
- Develop skills (via a more open exploration of the relational stances being adopted and how these impact their behaviour, and their enjoyment of life).
- Become more congruent with their lived experience.
- Become clearer about who they are and who they are not.
- Develop skills for managing anxiety.
- Learn to exercise choice authentically and responsibly.

Techniques that are Sensitive to Self and Others' Culture – Narrative Approaches

As mentioned in Chapter 3, approaches from narrative therapy have been 'transported' into coaching applications with some success (Law, 2007;

White, 1995a, 1997, 2000, 2006, 2007). In narrative coaching, we use 'story' as the metaphor to embody the coachee's lived experiences, for 'we tell ourselves stories in order to live' (Didion, 2006). And, if life is a story or the performance of that story (Myerhoff, 1982, 1986), then surely the first question in coaching is:

- What is your story?

Exercise 7.9

If the first coaching question is: What is your story? Then what do you think the steps of narrative coaching are? Make a list:

____

____

____

____

Like a story, we would expect the coaching conversation to have a sequence and structure along the storytelling:

1. Description – first invite the coachees to describe their story. This likely consists of a sequence of events. Like a story, it would have a time-line, structure, drama, themes, plots, key actors, backdrop, place, culture, circumstance and context (landscape of action).
2. Relation – the narrative coach would need to make sense of the coachee's description (storylines) in terms of the chains of association and relationship between those events (meaning-making frame).

The above sequence forms the first part of narrative coaching known as externalizing conversation. It provides you with a rich picture (understanding and insight) into the coachee's life, relationships, values, beliefs and self-identity. This is a starting point; it is not a complete coaching process. Some coachees may identify the solution themselves through the externalizing conversation and they would see the picture more clearly, separating themselves from the problems. Remember: the essence of externalizing conversation is that the problem is the problem (out there); and the coachee is not a problem. To complete the coaching process, you need to do re-authoring or re-membering (depending on the themes of the story), which are described next.

Re-authoring

Following the process of the externalizing conversation, re-authoring consists of three more stages:

1. Evaluation – as in coaching, the coach at a certain point invites the coachee to reflect on what has been said; about the story being told. The coach may ask the coachee to re-evaluate their action/s in relation to their values and beliefs, trying to make meaning from the story with the possibility of developing other alternative storylines. The awareness of the possible alternative storylines constitutes a new beginning of the story development (a 'turning point'). The further development of the alternative (and positive) storyline provides 'scaffolding' to bridge the existing gap between the story being told so far and the coachee's aspiration, hopes and dreams.
2. Justification – the coach asks the coachee to re-evaluate the outcomes of the story so far and how they relate to their own life and identity (mapping the landscape of action onto the landscape of their consciousness).
3. Conclusion/Recommendation – finally, the coach invites the coachee to conclude the conversation by developing an action plan that resonates with the coachee's values, beliefs and self-identity. The coach may ask the coachee to make an explicit valued statement about this.

Very often, the story being told may relate to one or more significant persons in relation to the coachee's life. If these people can have a positive influence upon the coachee's future development, then re-membering may be a good way to re-author the coachee's story.

Re-membering conversations

Re-membering may be regarded as a specific form of re-authoring. It does not mean remembering. Re-membering regards the social dimension of one's life as a 'membered' club in association with others as members (Myerhoff, 1980, 1986; White, 2006). Using this metaphor, it implies that one is free to re-group, and re-define the boundary of one's own club in relation to the others (members). One can re-define the membership, re-draw the boundaries of one's own associations by excluding certain members from the past, or including and recruiting new members into the club – hence the term re-membering. It is an active process of re-evaluating and re-defining one's life membership in association with other people.

From the above, we can see that, unlike other behavioural coaching approaches, narrative coaching does not only focus on solving a problem or issue resulting in identifying goals; more importantly, it focuses on the coachee's self-identity and their beliefs, values, hopes and dreams (landscape of consciousness). However, narrative coaching does involve having an action plan (though sometimes 'to do nothing' may be an appropriate option). The role of the coach in narrative coaching is MORE THAN a companion on the journey – they need to accomplish the following:

In the first phase, try to:

1. Make sense of the coachee's story by relationship mapping, and so on.
2. Listen to the story attentively to identify any positive but hidden storylines (which often appear in the background as thin traces).

At the turning point of the coaching conversation – moment of change:

- Help the coachee to re-structure their story into a more positive storyline – either using re-authoring or re-membering.

In the second phase, try to consolidate the development of the positive storyline by:

1. Ensuring that the new storyline is in alignment with the coachee's value, meaning and self-identity (as earlier) – to thicken the plot.
2. Inviting the coachee to think about the possible future action – again, link those actions/proposals back to the coachee's values, meanings and self-identity.

Questions towards the end of re-authoring may include:

- Coach: Having identified this (new story/new you), what will you do next?
- Coachee: I will do .... (this and that)...
- Coach: What does this action mean to you? Or
- How does this action resonate with your value that you expressed earlier (or your identity, who you are, and so on)?
- When will you do that?

Outsider witness re-telling and definitional ceremony

Narrative coaching may also be used in groups. In a group situation, we still have a coachee, but all other members act as a 'witness' to the coachee's story. The group member in this role provides extra support to the coachee, as their re-telling the coachee's story provides resonance that would amplify the coachee's strength and sense of identity.

Having listened to the coachee's story, the narrative coach invites the outsider witnesses to re-tell the story, guiding them to express the aspects of the story that touch their emotions. These aspects include:

- Expression (description) – identifying the key expressions that stuck to the outsider witness.
- Images – describe the image (re-tell the story – talk about what was heard).
- Resonances – embody responses – ensure the expressions resonate with the coachee's own experience (not just the witnesses' own experience).
- Catharsis – acknowledge transport; the way that they have been moved by the story and what they have learnt from the story that can apply to their own life.

The outsider witness approach can also be applied within groups, or for a whole organization or community. In this case, the outsider witness may re-tell the story of the re-told story and so on. This could take place in a whole-day conference (ceremony) or in a number of days for a local community. This application is known as 'definitional ceremony'.

Summary and reflection on narrative coaching

To sum up, narrative approaches enable coaches and coachees to elicit solution-focused, positive outcomes that contradict many of the negative conclusions that otherwise might have been reached by coachees if they were left to draw their own conclusions. These valued conclusions open possibilities for coachees to take action in relation to the previous problems and predicaments. They provide a foundation for the identification of unique positive outcomes.

The narrative approach provides a platform where participants tell stories. Through the dialogue between the storytellers and the active listeners, the storytellers find the opportunity to progressively distance themselves from their lives, and it is from this distance that they become *aware* about solutions to their problems. As a result of the conversation, the storytellers are re-invigorated to understand *what it is* that is happening, how it has happened, and what it all means. Note the importance of 'meaning', which is brought to the foreground through the narrative conversation. Narrative coaches encourage coachees to re-engage with their own meaning, resources, skills and knowledge in their life and history. This provides them with a foundation and options to move forward with their lives and relationships.

Finally, we have also 'transported' (in a transpersonal sense) our emotion to a state of new understanding with an acknowledgements to the coachees who share with us their personal story. Thus the definition ceremony is a powerful narrative procedure. It is applicable to a large group, conferences and communities across cultures. Readers may find that the practice is entirely new in the coaching arena. However, the concept relates to many strands of the ILS and psychology of learning, in particular the reflective element, which resonates throughout the narrative practice. For instance, the re-tellings by the outsider witnesses contribute significantly to the rich description of specific aspects of the stories of community members who told the story. These may link to the identification of the knowledge and skills by the storytellers during their reflection – re-telling of re-telling. The reflections may be on the storytellers' experiences of the re-telling itself, or on the images of life and identity that were evoked in the process. These reflections are characterized by the expression of significant realizations on personal, community and cultural identity, on shared purposes and values, and on the knowledge and skills that are grounded in their community and their personal histories.

Exercise 7.10

Having read the story of the narrative story, summarize the aim of narrative coaching.

What are the roles of a narrative coach?

What is the coaching attitude of a narrative coach?

What are the difficulties that a coach may encounter in narrative coaching; in outsider witness; and in definitional ceremony, respectively?

____

____

____

____

Putting it All Together – Principle of Empowerment Psychology for Coaching

From the coaching techniques you have studied so far, by now you may realize that there are some common processes that underpin all of them. This section describes a general model of coaching called the Empsy® Model of Coaching (EMC) from which you may be able to see how each technique can link to each individual stage of the process within the model.

EMC is based on the psychology of empowerment, which focuses on understanding of the individual's situation and mapping it with the appropriate strategies of intervention. The principle of EMC consists of two parts:

1. Model of situation.
2. Model of intervention.

Empsy® model of situation

The model examines the coachee's current situation and the process of its development. It takes a rich contextual situation as a starting point, and requires the coach to develop an insight and understanding of the issues embedded within it in terms of its:

1. Sources – external causal factors, such as physical environment, social and cultural factors.
2. Psychological factors – the individual's emotion and cognition.
3. Outcome – the behaviours, actions and consequences of those actions.
4. Feedback loop – the kind of feedback mechanism that may or may not strengthen the desired behaviours, thinking and belief.

The process of situation development can be represented in Figure 7.8.

In simple S–R psychology, a *source* may be regarded as a stimulus to an individual. Here, from the systems perspective, the sources represent all the possible inputs from a person's environment in a wider sense. For example, 'someone being horrible to me' can be a source of stress. This affects a person's state of mind and feeling (psychological factors). For example: 'I feel bad' as a result of being treated badly. He/she then behaves accordingly, e.g. starts shouting at other people (the outcome). In turn, that negative behaviour has an effect on others, who perceive the person negatively, e.g. 'He/she is aggressive', and respond negatively to the person as well. This forms a vicious circle, known as reinforcement in

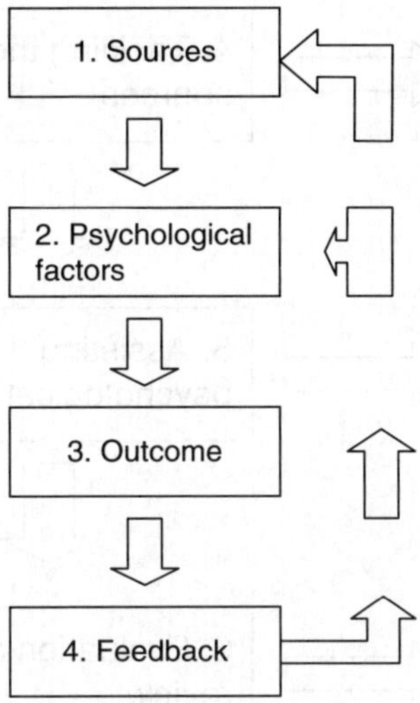

Figure 7.8 Process model of the situation analysis.

S-R psychology. However, in the Empsy® model, it is simply referred to as a feedback mechanism to include both positive and negative feedback loops.

Empsy® model of intervention

From the above model of situation, if we are to empower individuals and organizations to achieve their aspirations, we must tackle the situation at each stage of the process. This is essentially a solution-focused process and consists of the following stages (Figure 7.9):

1. Tackling the sources – identifying possible alternative actions and solutions.
2. Assisting psychological aspects.
3. Expecting new outcomes (evaluation, monitoring and review).
4. Further feedback (to consolidate the positive outcome).

We first tackle the sources, identifying which psychological states can become barriers. We then derive a strategy to assist the psychological aspects of the coachee. If the strategy works, we would expect new outcomes from both individuals and organizations. This in turn creates a new feedback loop due to a new pattern of social interaction. We need to continue to monitor and review the outcome, which forms an important part of any evidence-based evaluation. These cycles of events form the Empsy® model of coaching.

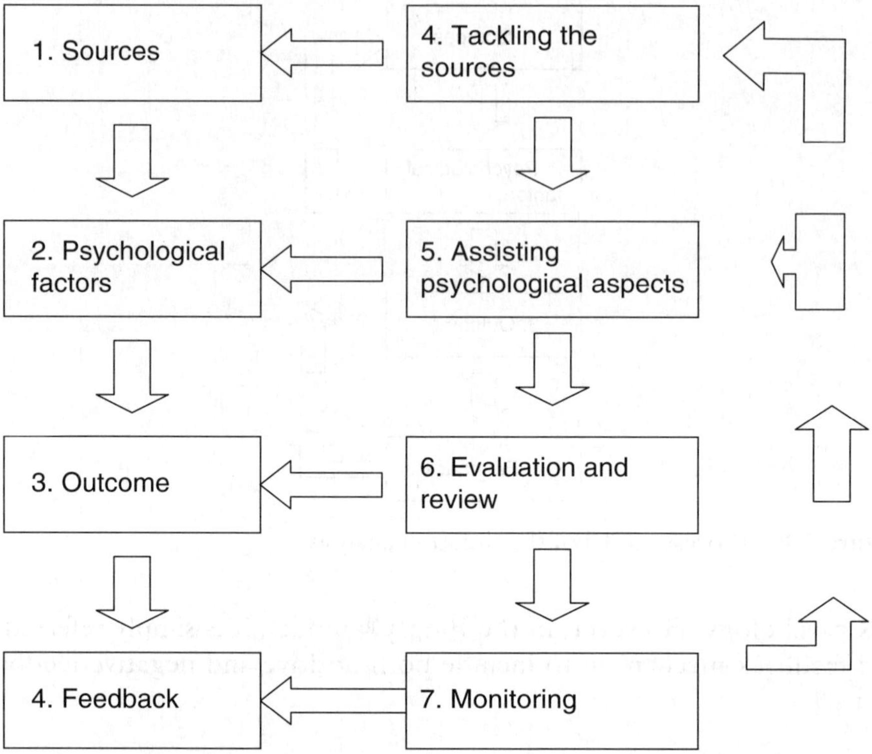

Figure 7.9 Empsy® model of coaching

Exercise 7.11

So far, you have acquired knowledge of a number of coaching techniques. Look at Figure 7.9 and select a technique that you may use at each stage of the cycle. Which techniques would you use to identify the sources that lead to the coachee's current situation, e.g. the existential or narrative approach? Which techniques would you use to tackle their psychological factors, e.g. self-limited belief that underlies their lack of confidence?

Make a list of possible techniques at each stage:

____

____

____

____

Chapter Summary and Reflection

In this chapter you have learnt a range of coaching approaches that can readily be 'plugged in' to the UIF/ILS framework. These include:

- gestalt techniques (including CBC)
- CBT (or CBC)
- existential approach (ABC model)
- narrative approaches (include both one-to-one and groups).

I hope that you have found the approaches range from organizational to transpersonal and interpersonal practice. They are a combination of:

- scientific–artistic orientation
- power and ordinariness
- 50% divine and 50% materialistic.

The role of the coaches within these approaches include the following:

- Facilitate change.
- Help produce optimal performance/well-being.
- Assess the situation and coachees' competence, learning or performance.
- Clarify thoughts, values, purposes, goals, aims and objectives.
- Provide guidance.
- Help discover/interpretive meaning.
- Facilitate narratives.
- Understand from the coachees' perspectives.
- Be part of the process. (The method cannot be separated from the coach as a person.)
- Work from within the relationship or system rather than bring a 'tried and tested' structure/model to bolt on to it.
- Work with 'what is'.
- Help the coachees to focus on here-and-now and to see what they are currently doing to create the blockage.
- Help the coachees to explore themselves in the here-and-now.
- Challenge coachees' assumptions, for example the way they relate to others.
- Encourage coachees to experiment with a new way of dealing with habits, for example in relationships.
- Ask the coachees to express something behaviourally rather than to talk and theorize about it, for example act or talk like P.

- Be aware of one's own top/underdog monologues.
- Encourage the externalization of the internal debate.
- Clarify and act as mediator in the struggle.
- Help coachees decide what they want to do and how.
- Help coachees figure out the unwritten rules and cultural codes of the dominance.
- Help coachees to find an informal mentor within or outside of the organization.
- Help coachees to identify their goals.
- Create a career or succession plan with your coachees.

You should by now understand that *to be* a coach implies a certain attitude in your practice. In gestalt psychology, 'to be' means an appreciation of:

- Actuality – To be present. To be there. To be here-and-now.
- Awareness – To be present as living and lived existence.
- Responsibility – To be responsible.

Enlightenment is not a state or a content of the mind, but mind, as such, is the container. For the narrative approach, the scaffolding is the container. Like an artist, the gestalt coach provides a form of coaching in practice:

Attitude =>form

This attitude is grounded in the awareness of one's experience in the here-and-now, which embodies the past and future as a moment for change. Like an artist, in all cases, the coach plays a facultative role (de-centred); it is the participant (the coachee) that engages with the art (the outcome) and takes the centre stage. The coach, like a tourist guide for the coachee's journey, must be an expert in the techniques. Practice makes perfection; Chapter 8 provides more exercises for practising the art.

8

Practical Exercises

Time to practise

Introduction

This chapter provides further useful exercises to help you to practise some of the techniques and tools described in Chapter 7. A few of these exercises can be practised on your own, while others are designed for you to work in pairs or groups. In particular, they will help you to:

- plan your coaching practice
- conduct coaching conversations (in one-to-one and/or group situations).

But first, let's review what you have learnt within the framework of the Integrative Learning System (ILS) and how this can be put into practice and advance your skills as part of your continuous professional development (CPD).

ILS Training and CPD

Exercise 8.1

Take another look at Figure 6.6 in Chapter 6, or your own model of coaching, examine each sub-system and element within the model. How can it be used for your CPD practice and supervision?

____

____

____

____

Writing and keeping a reflective log

Keeping a coaching log to reflect on your practice is an important element of your CPD. The Appendix at the end of this book provides you with a template for a reflective log. You can use this to record your practice as part of your CPD.

Exercise 8.2 Making your own CBC log

In Chapter 7, you learnt about a cognitive behavioural coaching (CBC) approach; have another look at Figure 7.3 (if necessary, re-read about the approach) and compare it with the template in the Appendix.

How would you embed the element of CBC in your reflective log?

____

____

____

____

Re-format your own CBC log if necessary.

Exercises in learning

Exercise 8.3 Identifying and developing a coaching intervention

Learning is a foundation for coaching. In Chapter 7, you learnt about the Empsy® model of coaching (see Figure 7.9).

Referring to the model, and thinking of a learning experience that you have had, try to:

1. identify sources of negative learning
2. identify possible psychological factors
3. develop an intervention strategy for your next coaching session, using the above.

____

____

____

____

Running a Coaching/Mentoring/Training Session

In this section I have provided a list of items/questions that you may find useful to consider when running a coaching and mentoring session. These are structured so that they fit logically into the following phases:

- beginning – preparation
- middle – during the session
- end of the session.

Preparation

Before carrying out any exercise, like conducting a coaching session, it is important for the coach/organizer to prepare for the environment of the session. The coach/trainer needs to ensure that the setting is safe and comfortable for the coachee to participate fully and freely. Before commencing the session, the coach/trainer should ensure that the space is suitable for the exercise to be undertaken, and that the venue meets the requirements of the Health & Safety at Work Act. Always check that there is a qualified first-aider on site and a first-aid kit available. For example, the following checklist provides items for the coach/trainer to take note:

- lighting
- heating/air-conditioning
- ventilation
- noise/acoustics
- seating
- general condition of venue
- electricity supply/sockets
- uneven or split floor surface
- entry and exits
- toilets/washing facilities
- refreshment-making facilities
- smoking/non-smoking areas
- first-aid facilities/equipment
- fire safety equipment
- fire escape procedure
- other safety measures
- other hazards
- in-house first-aid contact
- how to contact this person
- an adequate size room for the exercises
- adequate supervision for group exercises – coach/delegate ratio
- obstructions on the walls, radiators, light switches, low hanging light fittings or low ceilings.

In terms of their personal development, before the session the coach may ask him-/herself – what do I want my coachees to walk away from the coaching/mentoring session with? For the coachee, the question would be – what do I want to walk away from the coaching/mentoring session with?

Structuring coaching sessions – the first meeting with your potential coachee

As part of the preparation, it may be useful to prepare a 'script' for your first session. Consider how you would introduce yourself; your background (e.g. qualifications and experiences); the code of ethics (as discussed

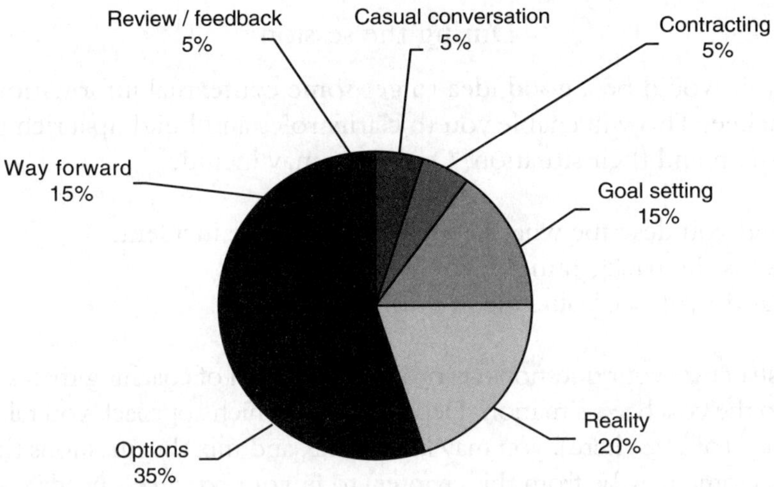

Figure 8.1 Timing of a session

in Chapter 2; including professional boundaries, limited confidentiality, informed consent on note taking and record keeping); the coaching contract (including the legal aspects, frequency and length of the session, fees and cancellation policies); your coaching approach, and so on.

According to a general coaching process, it is likely that you will cover the following items in a session:

- Discuss (or review) a coaching contract and the individual's understanding of arrangements.
- Ask the coachee what they want to achieve from the coaching process (goal/s).
- Work to build the relationship.
- Agree an agenda (two/three sessions).
- Begin work on the goal/s.
- Monitor the time.
- Set the coachee an assignment towards the end of the session.
- Review any achievements of the goals.

You may like to plan and divide your session according to your model of practice. For example, for a coaching model like GROW, people tend to spend various amounts of time on each stage of the process as shown in Figure 8.1.

The exact amount of time at each stage may vary in different situations; but it would be a good idea to plan roughly how you will divide the time of your session and agree with the coachee in advance.

During the session

Initially, it would be a good idea to get some contextual information from the coachee. This will enable you to clarify roles and build up a rich picture about them and their situation. Questions may include:

- Could you describe what happened during the incident?
- What is the background?
- What do you see your role as in this?

Try to structure your questions according to a model of coaching that is appropriate to the coachee's situation. Depending on which approach you take from Chapter 7 (or elsewhere), you may like to pick and mix the questions that you develop (some may be from this chapter) to fit your coachee's needs.

End of session

At the end of the session, it is important for the coach/mentor to formally or informally evaluate the feelings of the coachee. Ask for feedback regarding their perceptions of the session. Questions may include:

- What has this session been like for you?
- How was this for you?
- How do you feel about this?
- Where do you stand on this?
- What is your position on this?
- Is this a positive or negative development, both, or neither of these?
- How do you feel about this development?
- How come you're taking this stand/position on this development?
- Is this okay with you?

After the session

After the session, try to reflect upon your learning. For example:

- What were you thinking/feeling during the engagement/incident?
- What went well?
- In the light of what happened, would you have done anything differently?
- What else could you have done?
- If a similar situation arose again, what would you do?
- What are you going to do to further improve and develop yourself/your performance?

Writing the reflection explicitly (using the reflective log described earlier) will help you to learn and develop your practice further. The rest of the chapter provides some exercises for you to practise the techniques that you have learnt. These include:

- NLP coaching exercises.
- Gestalt/mindfulness exercises.
- Existential exercises.
- Narrative/storytelling exercises.

NLP Coaching Exercises

Meta model exercise

In Chapter 7, you learnt about the NLP meta model. If you can, try to observe a coaching session as a group (triad). Monitor the coach–coachee dialogue during the coaching session. Write down your observations in Columns 3 and 4 of Table 8.1 as appropriate.

After the observation, think about what you would say if you were the coach. Write down your answers (coaching questions) in Column 5.

Anchoring

In this section, you will be able to acquire the skills of anchoring following a set of step-by-step procedures. Having learned the basic steps of anchoring in principle, you can apply this procedure to help you gain more resources or help your coachees to overcome their fear.

Anchoring resources

You can use anchoring to your advantage by deliberately associating with a specific and useful resource to any stimulus you choose. To do this, simply apply the three-step anchoring technique as follows:

1. Generate the resource state (R_1) – create within yourself the particular set of feelings which you want to use as a resource, e.g. confidence.
2. Calibrate your resource state (R_1), using your physiology as a cue.
3. Set new anchors (S_1) – choose a convenient stimulus in one or more sensory systems (i.e. something you see, hear or feel) and use it as your anchor to associate it with all your feelings and experiences in (R_1).

Table 8.1 NLP meta model exercise

1. Language pattern	*2. Description*	*3. Coachee's statement (observed)*	*4. Coach's response (Q) (observed)*	*5. Your coaching questions*
Deletions:				
Simple deletion	Information is missing E.g. They do … Q: '*Do what?*'			
Unspecified comparatives	Comparison is not explicit as to whom or what it is being compared: '…*than what or whom?*' E.g. I performed better yesterday. Q: *Compared with whom or when?*			
Unspecified verb	How is not specified: *How specifically?* E.g. She taught herself … Q: *How did she teach herself?*			
Unspecified referential index **(pronoun)**	Does not specify who it refers to E.g. They learn it quickly. Q: *Who learns?* *Who specifically?*			
Lost performative	Value judgement – by whom? '*Who says?*' E.g. It's wrong to bad mouth people. Q: *Who says so? How do you know it is wrong?*			

Distortions:	
Nominalization	When verbs turn into nouns E.g. His performance is poor. Q: *How could he perform better?*
Cause and effect	Implying one thing causes another, but the actual causal mechanism is not specified: x causes y to happen. How does x cause y? E.g. You irritate me. Q: *How specifically do I irritate you?*
Presupposition	Making assumptions, which have been taken for granted E.g. I will enjoy learning this. Q: *What is the assumption here?*
Mind reading	Claiming to know someone's thoughts E.g. David is miserable. Q: *How do you know? What leads you to believe that?*
Complex equivalence	Implying two things are equal. X ⇔ Y '*How does x mean y?*' E.g. You never listen to me (pause) You never provide eye contact. Q: *So not providing eye contact means I am not listening to you? How, specifically, does providing the eye contact mean listening?*

(*Continued*)

Table 8.1 (*Cont'd*)

1. Language pattern	*2. Description*	*3. Coachee's statement (observed)*	*4. Coach's response (Q) (observed)*	*5. Your coaching questions*
Generalizations:				
Universal quantifiers	All, every, etc. E.g. All NLP courses are too expensive. Q: *ALL NLP courses are too expensive? Which one specifically? Are there any exceptions to that?*			
Modal operator of possibility	Might, could, etc. E.g. I can't get myself organized. Q: *What would happen if you did? What stops you? What would happen if you could?*			
Modal operator of necessity	Must, should, etc. E.g. I shouldn't interrupt when people are talking. Q: *What would happen if you did? What stops you?*			

Practise the above three steps until you can use your anchor (S_1) to summon this state (R_1) at will. That is, whenever you create your anchor (S_1) you experience it as if you were in R_1 state. An association is formed between the resource state (R_1) and the selected anchor (S_1). Resource anchoring works best when you build associations between the desired emotional state (R_1) and anchor (S_1) in more than one sensory stimulus. We would recommend you to use three (3-tuple), say: visual, auditory and kinaesthetic (V^i, A^d and K^i), depending on your sensory preference. For example: imagine choosing a piece of stone that you collected during your holiday at the seaside as your positive anchor (S_1). You choose it perhaps because it reminded you of the experience that you had when you were in that place – you felt so free, calm, yet wild and creative.

Whenever you hold and *touch* this piece of stone in your hand (**K**inaesthetic), you could *see* the picture (**V**isual) of the sea, and you could hear the sound of the waves (**A**uditory).

This piece of stone has become your magical stone. You may choose to carry it to attend interviews, for example; whenever you feel anxious, just hold this stone in your hand. It instantly transports you to that beautiful place where you were so calm, free and imaginative.

Exercise 8.4

Practise the three-step anchoring to gain the resources that are relevant to your own life. What anchors have you identified?

____

____

____

____

Dissociation

The first stage to change any undesirable anchors (S–R) such as phobias or traumatic experiences is 'dissociation'. This change pattern takes the following steps:

1. Establish a 'bail-out' anchor (S_1–R_1) – this is achieved by using the three-step anchoring technique discussed earlier. First, identify a positive state

(R_1) that you prefer to the negative state (R_0). The positive state can be a 'here and now' state. Secondly, calibrate R_1, and then thirdly, anchor R_1 by selecting a new stimulus (S_1) and associating it with the positive state (R_1).

2. Calibrate the external physiology of the anchor (R_0) with the state of the negative anchor (S_0) – for instance, in post-traumatic stress disorder after a car accident, a picture of a car may be associated with the traumatic experience. Be sure your coachee accesses this anxiety state minimally. For instance, anchor the phobia by finding the earliest scene before the accident.
3. Re-pair the old pattern (S_0–R_1) – shake out the negative anchor and its negative associations (S_0–R_0). Re-anchor S_0 with the positive state (R_1). For instance, instruct your coachee to imagine that they are about to go through the scene on a video so as to comfortably see the scene for the purpose of learning from it.

Note the above procedure is effectively a recursion of the standard three-step anchoring technique. Of course, in practice, it may be more complicated. Your coachee may require a lot of practice of the new skills. For instance, using the same example as above, you may first guide the coachee to imagine that they are watching the video in black and white; but have it go backwards. Ensure you start from a time when they knew they were 'safe' after the accident, and finish at a time when they knew they were 'safe' before the accident. Then run the video forwards. Do this quickly so the conscious mind does not have too much time to dwell on anything. If there is any collapse of their state towards the phobic state immediately stop the video and make whatever change is necessary before continuing. For example, change sensory sub-modalities (S') or add resources (R'). As the coachee is watching the 'scene', guide them to use the new anchor S_1 (e.g. if 'here and now' is the R_1 state, then instruct them to have a 'here and now' dialogue with their new (or so-called 'younger') self about the experience for the purpose of learning. At each step, as you notice through calibration that they are retaining a positive emotional state, then begin to add more richness to the scene (e.g. colour and smell as appropriate to that journey). If necessary, slow down the video so they become more conscious and can learn fully about the experience.

When the coachee feels they are happy with the above learning, test your work and see what happens when you try to anchor the phobia again (i.e. repeat Step 2). If the work is not complete, then repeat the practice and provide more resources as necessary.

Gestalt Exercises

The essence of gestalt techniques is to increase your awareness about the present – the here-and-now – moment. A lot of gestalt exercises are known as mindfulness exercises, which are very similar to meditation practice in the

Exercise 8.5 Presence

This exercise focuses on the sense of presence. It can be done alone, in pairs or in a group. If working in pairs, ask each pair to sit face to face – and close their eyes. Then follow these instructions:

1. Stop doing what you are doing.
2. Close your eyes.
3. Be quiet.
4. Breathe in.
5. Pause.
6. Breathe out.
7. Be as you want to be.
8. Pay attention to your bodily sensations, posture and facial expression.
9. Make any necessary adjustment in your posture based on your awareness, moment by moment.
10. Place your tongue against your upper palate.
11. Focus on your sense of taste.
12. Swallow your saliva.
13. What does it taste like?
14. Now focus on your smell as you breathe in and out…
15. What can you smell?
16. Now focus on your internal sensations.
17. Can you feel the sensation from your stomach?
18. Feel your heart beat…
19. Be aware of your breathing.
20. When you feel comfortable and ready, open your eyes while remaining still.
21. Relax your body.
22. Relax your eyes.
23. Pay attention to what is going on around you – the movements, sights and sounds…
24. Be aware of the ebb and flow of your consciousness of the sensations.

East. One would argue that mindfulness practice is actually based on Buddhism. Within this tradition, the terms 'psychology and mindfulness' are not used – they are the Western packaging. Having imported the ideas and practices from the East, they were then reintegrated to the gestalt psychology. As it turns out, the two do go hand-in-hand. For instance, both gestalt psychology and Buddhism emphasize the focus of the present moment/experience; and some advanced analytical meditation involves understanding the human perception, which is consistent with the gestalt psychology. For further discussion on the mindfulness debate, see Law (2012).

The following exercises will help you to increase your self-awareness.

Existential exercises

In existential coaching, there are three key points to remember:

1. Be fully aware of the presence about yourself and your coachees.
2. Try to make sense (the meaning) of the coachees' descriptions (like narrative approach).
3. Try to help the coachees understand that they are the agents who have autonomy and responsibility to make choices for themselves and others, and that all choices are of equal value (i.e. you do not prescribe your own value to those choices that the coachee makes).

So to be fully present, you might like to try out some mindfulness exercises described earlier; here is another one within the existential context about one's perception of time.

Exercise 8.6 Stopping time

Try this mindfulness exercise to be aware of the time and the present moment:

1. Stop doing what you are doing.
2. Close your eyes.
3. Focus on your being here-and-now.
4. Be quiet.
5. Breathe in.

6. Pause.
7. Breathe out.
8. Keep doing this breathing exercise until you feel that you are ready to begin the next step, and then open your eyes.
9. Pay attention to what is going on around you – the movements, sights and sounds…
10. Now pay attention to your own body – its position, tensions…
11. Focus on your thoughts.
12. Feel your sense of the present, right here, right now.
13. Imagine there is no time…
14. There is only this moment.
15. Be aware that everything is just as it is.
16. Time stops.

Exercise 8.7 Existential coaching

Conduct a coaching conversation with your coachee using the existential approach. Try to observe the following rules:

1. The rule of epoche – try to be non-judgemental without having any assumptions, pre-conceived ideas or prejudice about your coachee. Be fully present. Conduct a mindfulness exercise described in the previous section if it helps.
2. The rule of description – invite your coachee to tell you about their experience concerning their recent significant event (something positive), e.g. what have they learnt. Ask 'what' and 'how' (but not 'why') questions. For example, what was it like to be ….?
3. The rule of horizontalization – invite the coachee to make a choice at the option stage. Give equal value to each option.

Reflect on and describe your experience afterwards. What was it like to coach with the existential approach? Write a reflective log about your experience.

____

____

____

____

Narrative/Storytelling Exercises

Narrative approaches consist of the following techniques:

- externalizing conversation
- re-authoring conversation
- re-membering conversation
- group exercises: outsider witness re-telling and definitional ceremony (re-tellings of re-tellings).

Below are some examples of narrative questions that you may find useful in your exercises:

- Would you tell me a story about your life that would help me to understand why you would take this position on this development?
- Does the kind of work you do reflect your values, beliefs, aspirations, hopes and dreams?
- What are your values, beliefs, aspirations, hopes and dreams?
- How do you establish those criteria that enable you to measure the success of achieving your aspirations, hopes and dreams?
- Why do you feel/think this way?
- If this experience was uncomfortable to you, what would you do?
- In order to clarify your concern, could you give it a name?
- What new information are you taking in?
- How would you look at this from different perspectives?
- In what way are you trying new ways of thinking, feeling and doing?
- How would you integrate these new ways of thinking or being into your life?
- You reached this conclusion without much hesitation. Can you think of any events of your life that would reflect this conclusion?

Exercise 8.8 Learning about description

The intention with this exercise is to give you a better sense and understanding of your own learning engagement using externalizing conversation. Please follow these instructions (15–20 minute conversation).

- Work in pairs (coach and coachee).
- As a narrative coach, please take notes during the conversation (remember: ask for permission first).

Use the following questions as a guideline for your dialogue with the coachee:

- Opening question: 'Can you describe a situation from your recent work or private life where you really feel that you have learned something new or special?'
- Possible probing questions:
  - What happened to you in this situation?
  - What kind of support did you receive from outside?

Tasks during the listening:

- Identify some main constituents that you consider as the basis for a fruitful learning process.

After the conversation: reflect on the key learning that your coachee has had.

Exercise 8.9 Learning about relationship mapping

The intention with this exercise is to give you a sense of how you can develop an in-depth relationship to a specific situation. Please follow these instructions (15–20 minute conservation).

- Work in pairs (coach and coachee).
- Use the following questions as a guideline for your dialogue with the client:
  - Please choose a specific situation which has been important for you…
  - How do you perceive the situation?
  - How would you describe it?
  - What more can you describe?
  - Can you find a metaphor or picture for your felt sense?

Tasks during the listening:

- Identify the coachee's aspirations, values, hopes and dreams that give them a sense of purpose.
- How did these hopes and dreams reflect in the story (are they 'thin' or 'thick' descriptions)?
- What is the gap, if any, between the coachee's aspiration and their description?

Make a note on the key challenges that you and your coachee have had.

Externalizing conversation

Externalizing conversation consists of two steps:

1. Description – the coachee describes their story.
2. Relation – establish chains of association and relationships between those events, and make meaning of them.

The following exercises will help you to practise the above steps.

Exercise 8.10 Externalizing conversation using a reflective log

Working with your coachee, use the reflective log template to guide your conversation. Complete steps 1–3.

1. (Description) Invite your coachee to tell a story about their positive learning experience (or a coaching topic that they would like to discuss). This may consist of events that have recently happened to them; or from the distant past. Ask them to try to give their story a name/title.
2. Having noted your coachee's feelings and thoughts (as well as your own), try to think about what theme/plot these emotions and thoughts would fit in the coachee's storyline.
3. Invite the coachee to reflect on how the above storyline resonates with their aspirations, beliefs, values, hopes and dreams. What was the unique outcome, if any? Are there any gaps between what happened and what they would have liked to happen? What was the desirable outcome? How do all these relate to their sense of self-identity?

Re-authoring conversation

Like other coaching approaches, re-authoring is future focused. It aims to redevelop coachees' skills and knowledge by redeveloping the alternative stories of their life experience. In re-authoring, the coachee's story is regarded as a 'script', and the coachee the 'author'. As such, the coachee should have the power and freedom to re-author the story of their life. Here one can regard re-authoring as another form of externalization – where the coachee is taking an externalized position to view their 'life story' as an author.

The process of re-authoring is collaborative. The co-construction (co-authorship) of the alternative story is achieved by both the coachee and coach in equal partnership. This new story is filled with possibilities instead of the 'problem-full' old story (Bor and Legg, 2003). Here the role of the coach is to facilitate the conversation. The facilitation gives privileges to certain alternative accounts of the client's lived experience that are judged to be more desirable (e.g. positive).

In re-authoring, the narrative discourse of the coachee's beliefs and values are regarded as 'restraints' where a particular storyline has been chosen

Exercise 8.11 Re-authoring conversation

Continue the externalizing conversation exercise with the same coachee and use the same reflective log to guide your conversation.

Revisit Step 3 and complete the rest of the log:

- In Step 3, instead of asking the coachee to reflect further on what happened previously because of this and that, ask them to try to think about any exceptions to these unique outcomes of the events. What were the differences between these stories – the desirable and non-desirable ones? Questions may include:
    - Were there occasions that things happened better than or the same as you wished it to be?
    - What happened then?
    - Could you think of any other alternative situation?
    - What do you need to do to make the desirable unique outcome happen – in terms of resources, learning new skills, and so on?

Write them down in your log.

- In Step 4 (Evaluation), identify the gaps to reach the ideal unique outcome that resonates most with the coachee's strengths, beliefs, values and identity. Identify all the requirements that they need to get there. Questions may include:
    - What do you need to get there?
    - How will you acquire them?
    - Who could help you?
    - Where could you find them?
- In Step 5 (Conclusion), summarize the learning in Step 4. Invite the coachee to write down a statement of commitment for change that resonates strongly with their beliefs, values and identity.
- In Step 6 (Action Plan), together draw out a plan that consists of steps that the coachee needs to take next in order to achieve the desirable unique outcome.

'instead of' many possible alternatives. This concept of 'restraints' rather than 'cause' ('because of') is fundamental to re-authoring (read Bateson, 1972: 399 and Bor and Legg, 2003: 270 for further references).

As you may have noticed from the above exercises, re-authoring conversations provide opportunities (points of entry) for coachees to consider the new possibilities and actions about their lives in the near future (the landscapes of action). Thus the re-authoring questions were designed to help the coachees to develop alternative (new) accounts of the circumstances and proposals for action. In doing so, the narrative coach helps the coachee to scaffold the rich story development in their 'landscape of consciousness' which maps upon their landscapes of action.

At first, participants are likely to respond to landscapes of consciousness questions by talking about various categories of their self-identity, such as attributes, characteristics, deficits, drives, motives, needs, resources, strengths and traits. However, these conclusions may provide an inadequate basis for the coachees to proceed. In other words, they get stuck. Narrative coaches need to guide the storytellers with alternative identities that are more positive and relevant to the empowerment of their lives. Try to discover the storytellers' beliefs, commitments, intentions, purposes, values, visions, hopes and dreams.

Re-membering conversation

While re-authoring can be regarded as part of the externalizing conversation (a twist in the story development); re-membering can be regarded as a form of re-authoring when significant people ('actors') are involved in the coachee's story ('drama'). As a narrative coach, you can help your coachees to mobilize their human resources (the significant people) in relation to themselves to leverage positive change. So in a way re-membering adds a new dimension (human dimension) and complexity (an extra twist) to the story development, and requires skills of the coach to navigate the story development.

Group exercise: outsider witness re-telling

Outsider witness re-telling can be used in small or large groups. In this situation, as the coachee is telling his/her story, the other members in the group act as observers (outsider witnesses). After the coaching session, the observers will then be invited to recount their experience of listening to the story. The key questions for the outsider witnesses include:

1. Identifying the expression – What have you heard? Which expressions struck a chord for you?

Exercise 8.12 Re-membering conversation

Repeat the externalizing and re-authoring conversation exercises with either the same or different coachee. Start by inviting your coachee to tell a story about their positive learning experience; an event that recently happened to them; or something from the distant past. However, for the purpose of this exercise, ask them to think about a significant event that included people who are important to them. During the externalizing conversation stage, ask the coachee to richly describe this person (say X), so that you get a sense of how this person looks and their character. For example:

- What is his or her name?
- When, where and how did you meet?
- How would you describe this person?

In the re-authoring stage, try to encourage the coachee to:

- Recount the contributions of these significant figures (say X) to the coachee's life.
- Explain how these contributions helped to shape the coachee's identity?

Your questions may include:

- How did X help you?
- What did X bring to your life?
- How did it contribute to your success?
- In what way has it helped to become who you are?
- What kind of person do you think X would have perceived you to be?
- If X were here with you now, what do you think X would say about you?

And then swap the role of contribution between X and the coachee in your narrative questioning, i.e. ask the coachee to:

- Recount the coachee's contribution to X's life.
- Explain how these contributions helped to shape X's identity?

Your questions may include:

- What do you think you have brought to X's life?
- What have you added?
- What kind of person do you perceive X to be?
- If X were here with you now, what would you say to him/her?

Exercise 8.13 Group exercise – outsider witness re-telling

Another way (a simplified version) to do outsider witness re-telling in a group exercise (Stelter and Law, 2009) is called roundabout conversation. Select a topic. For example, you may choose to share an experience of appreciation, valuing an initiative taken and the development of alternative stories in a group (e.g. having done the narrative coaching exercises described earlier, you may decide to choose something entirely new).

Person A starts to present a situation where she has received positive appreciation, person B gives an appreciative feedback and relates the situation to his own experiences and invites person C to continue, and so on.

Ask a volunteer to share a story about his/her life/work, and swap seats with the participant sitting at your left. Ask the person the following questions:

1. What kind of words, phrases or expressions have caught your attention?
2. How did YOU perceive this word, phrase and expression? What are your feelings about it?
3. What kind of images about this person's life, identity and values do you get?

Reflection:

- What are the key differences of this exercise with the classic outsider witness approach mentioned in Chapter 7?
- In this case, who are the coachees?
- What are the advantages and disadvantages of this approach?
- When would you use this approach?

2. Describing the image – What images are evoked in your mind? How did these expressions or images help you to understand beliefs, commitments purposes, values, hopes, and dreams? Which are....?
3. Embodying responses – How does the coachee's story resonate with your own life/work?
4. Acknowledging transport – How do you feel having listened to the coachee's story? Has it moved you in any way (if so, how)? What have you learnt? In what way has the coachee's story contributed to your own learning and development? How would you like to acknowledge

this learning/experience that you have received (like a 'gift') in the presence of the coachee right here and now? What would you say to him/her in acknowledgement?

A final twist of outsider re-telling that is very often missed by narrative practitioners in training is that having listened to all the re-tellings of the story, the coachee is invited back by the coach to recount their experience of listening to their own story being re-told. Thus to conclude, the coachee is the last outsider witness of their own story. The purpose of this is to amplify the coachee's new (positive) story development (and commitment to action) even further. Moreover, the coachee is maintained at the centre of the narrative process. In other words, the coachee is the first and the last author of their own story.

Chapter Summary

In this chapter you have come across a range of exercises that you can practise in terms of coaching techniques and models. Practice makes perfect. Practising these exercises will help you to improve your coaching skills and to apply your coaching model and techniques seamlessly in your coaching conversation. Keeping a coaching log will enable you to learn further through reflection, and, over time, to accumulate a portfolio of case studies of your own that strengthen your practice. Chapter 9 examines a sample of case studies to illustrate the learning.

9

Collecting Your Own Successful Stories

Building a database of good practice

Introduction

As a professional practitioner in coaching psychology, you are encouraged to keep your own reflective log as part of your own learning and CPD. Chapter 8 provides guidance on how this may be achieved (with a template included in the Appendix). Whether the work is one to one, or a contract for a large organization, each log is a case study in its own right. Case studies are valuable for learning and CPD (Passmore *et al.*, 2011). Benefits include:

- increased awareness
- refined ethical framework
- developed case conceptualization
- explored beliefs and values
- continued learning.

This chapter provides a few case studies (based on Law, 2013) as examples to demonstrate the learning. These include:

- Leadership coaching and mentoring programmes for the healthcare system (Case Studies 1 and 2).
- E-coaching – a transatlantic coaching pilot project (Case Study 3).
- Coaching in communities (Case Studies 4 and 5).

Case Study 1 Leadership Coaching Project (UK)

Description

The coaching project was part of a leadership development programme within the healthcare sector in the UK. It aimed to empower the unrepresented black and minority ethnic (BME) staff and facilitators for organization change with coaching tools so that they could progress to senior levels and promote good practice. My role was as an external consultant to provide the delegates with the coaching training.

The process

The participants were selected for the leadership programme based on their personal profile (which provided details of their performance and demographic data). At the beginning of the process, selected delegates were asked to sign contracts and to agree on the code of ethics and expectations about their engagement (both during and after the completion of the training). They were then provided with a five-day coaching training course. The training included the introduction of the UIF coaching framework and a range of related coaching techniques (described in Chapters 6 and 7, respectively) and some practical exercises (as exemplified in Chapter 8). After the training, they were encouraged to apply their coaching techniques back into their workplace as a coach or mentor or a change agent and continue their supervsion as part of their CPD.

Cognition and emotion

Reflecting on my own thoughts and feelings, I was feeling quite excited by the opportunity to apply the coaching model that I was developing at the time to use it for promoting equality and diversity of leadership as part of the organization's change agenda. I was also apprehensive … Although I had some experience in the health sector a few years ago; working with leaders in the sector in coaching was new to me as well as for the participants. I think they were equally apprehensive too and wondered what coaching was all about and what I had to say during those five days.

Exercise 9.1

If you were one of the participants selected on the programme, how would you feel? And what would you be thinking about?

____

____

____

____

If you were one of the consults on the team delivering the coaching project, how would you feel? And what would you be thinking about?

____

____

____

____

Reflection

The feedback from the stakeholders of the programme suggested that coaching had significant benefits for both the individuals who participated in the training, and the organization which supported the programme. However, these benefits came quite a few months after the coaching training. The benefits include:

- The performance of the BME leaders who had the coaching training was significantly higher than the others.
- Fifty per cent of the delegates after the training programme were promoted.
- The senior management team benefited from the BME mentor who had acquired the coaching skills and knowledge.
- Coaching and mentoring had become embedded in the organizational culture. The process was consistent with that described by Clutterbuck and Megginson (2005).

Learning

The lessons learnt from the project at the organizational level include:

- Strategic planning for any coaching project to ensure sustainability is important.
- Partnership (strategic alliance) can help share resources to maintain the coaching culture and its sustainability.

Exercise 9.2 Reflecting on the delivery of your own coaching project

How well do you think the process has been delivered?

What went well and what did not go so well?

How do you understand the beliefs, values and experiences of the coachees and the coach; how have their self-values and concepts impacted on them during this project, and how did they transform the coaching outcome?

____

____

____

____

What have you learnt from the above project?

If you were asked to deliver a similar coaching project, what would you do to further improve and develop it? Write an action plan.

____

____

____

____

Case Study 2 Action Research for a Leadership Coaching Programme in Malta

The leadership coaching programme is a pilot for introducing coaching culture to a hospital in Malta. It aimed to show how a leadership coaching culture may be developed for nursing staff in a general hospital. Within this broad aim, we also hoped through the project that we could:

- identify the perceived idealized leadership attributes (ILA)
- identify the skill gap in leadership
- inform the management on how to implement a comprehensive coaching programme
- identify the impact of the programme.

My role was as supervisor for the manager who was responsible for the implementation of the pilot study. The manager was also a coach for the programme delivery.

The process

Twelve ward managers (seven females, five males, age range 32–46) were randomly selected to participate in the programme. They were provided with four one-to-one coaching sessions. The coaching model was based on the GROW model (Whitmore, 2002) with a range of eclectic techniques embedded in each stage as appropriate. The process of implementation followed an action research learning cycle:

1. planning
2. action
3. reflection.

The above stages were iterated in two phases: Phase 1 focused on getting the agreement and commitment from the Director of Nursing, selecting the coachees and conducting a focus group to identify ILA. Phase 2 focused on refining the implementation of the programme and providing feedback to the stakeholders.

Reflection

The GROW model with a 360-degree feedback process seemed to be useful to help coachees to achieve their goal. The coaching tools that were used within the process need to be refined so that they can be embedded in the coaching process more seamlessly. The themes identified from the focus group include: intrinsic values; vision; visibility and assertiveness. From these, numerous ILA were identified: authenticity; responsibility; collaboration; caring; excellence; safety; empowerment; influence; growth; vision; visibility; contribution; patience; inspiration; determination; courage; orderliness; appreciation; creativity; humility; diligence; pragmatism; prudence; reputation; ambition; meticulousness and conformity.

From the feedback of the participants, coaching helped them to increase their knowledge of leadership, and become aware of their strengths and areas of development. To further develop a coaching culture within the organization, it needs to consist of the following activities:

- formal coaching training
- individual coaching
- group coaching.

As a result of the coaching programme, there was a noticeable behavioural change in terms of the interdisciplinary documentation; the standard operating procedures; medication distribution systems and training programs development. The learning of the process was further documented and disseminated to various conferences and publications (see Aquilina and Law, 2012; Law and Aquilina, 2013).

Exercise 9.3 Reflecting on the action research

You may like to conduct the same reflective exercise by comparing and contrasting two recent coaching projects that you have carried out:

What are the similarities and differences between the two?

What are the cross-cultural themes embedded within the process?

How did these cultural themes impact upon the success of the programme?

How would you evaluate the success of the coaching programme?

____

____

____

____

Case Study 3 E-Coaching Across Cultures

This project was part of an international coaching initiative organized by members of the Association for Coaching (AC) in the UK (coordinator) to provide the leadership students at Rice University, Houston, Texas, with one-to-one coaching sessions via email and telephone or Skype. My role was one of the 20 selected coaches within AC to provide the coachee with the necessary coaching support. The project aimed to:

- inspire the students
- improve students' learning experience
- leverage students' leadership potential
- help students to develop themselves
- help students to become aware of cultural aspects of others as well as their own
- learn from the experience of e-coaching across cultures
- learn from the experience of working with high potential achievers
- improve the overall organizational performance of the university
- help the university to become familiar with coaching
- promote AC
- facilitate coaching research
- increase the knowledge and popularity of coaching
- support its members to take part in the international project.

Exercise 9.4 E-coaching across cultures

The project represents the complexity in implanting e-coaching internationally with multiple stakeholders. From the above list of aims, you can probably see that there are a number of different and competing aims from different stakeholders. Try to identify them and group the different objectives to different stakeholders.

____

____

____

____

The process

The students were provided with a coach and were entitled to request a coaching session over a 12-week period (total number of coaching sessions: 12 hours maximum). The coaching process was coachee led. In other words, it was up to the coachee to approach the coach to arrange a mutually convenient time to talk. The evaluation was carried out by the AC coordinator using a survey method with questionnaires at four regular intervals before, during and after the programme (Bresser, 2006a, b).

Exercise 9.5 The e-coaching process

What difficulties and challenges would you expect in coaching using electronic means such as telephone, Skype, Internet, and so on?

How would you overcome them?

What are the advantages and disadvantages in e-coaching in comparison with face-to-face coaching?

How would you evaluate such an e-coaching programme?

____

____

____

____

Evaluation

The results showed that coaching:

- added value to the students' studies
- increased students' self-awareness and reflection
- helped students to develop their thoughts
- helped students to get wider perspectives (think 'outside the box').

Interestingly, the virtual platform made some coachees feel 'safer' in terms of confidentiality. However, there were also other coachees who preferred face-to-face communication to conversation over the phone or Skype.

According to the feedback, the e-coaching programme could be further improved by:

- having coaching during term time
- providing more information (guidance) at the beginning of the programme
- providing help in scheduling the coaching sessions, taking account of the different time zones.

Excluding the 24 per cent 'don't know' responses, all the respondents rated the coaching as 'good' or 'very good'. Sixty-six per cent of the coachees believed that the continuous provision of the coaching support would increase the attractiveness of the university as 'a place to study'.

Case Study 4 Narrative Coaching in Communities

This was a local community project funded by the government in the UK (the Home Office). It was part of the UK-wide programme called the 'Positive Image' with the aim to empower marginalized individuals in local communities. The project in Peterborough was led by Peterborough Racial Equality Council (PREC) and delivered by its partners. My company was one of the partners and I was responsible for delivering the coaching project with an objective to develop positive 'role models' within the local communities. The major outputs of the project included:

- three-day coaching training sessions for community leaders and practitioners
- three community group gatherings
- a community conference
- a project report
- publication of an e-journal.

The process

I used the narrative approach (definitional ceremony) for this particular project because it is particularly useful for promoting the integration of the participants into the local community by sharing their personal stories of hardship and survival, and celebrating their contributions to the cultural and socioeconomic life of their host countries.

The coaching project also provided workshops and training prior to the conferences, involving the selected participants and the local networks, primarily from Peterborough and some from the neighbouring areas. The community conference was a step on a path for highlighting the revised social and political interventions and to induce public and private institutions to listen to real desires, needs and will of the marginalized communities, introducing their point of view through their personal and collective narratives. The conference lasted a whole day with the participation of many local organizations, charities and the city council as well as a representative from the Home Office.

Most of the selected participants were marginalized community members, travellers, new immigrants and refugees from different cultures. They were provided with a three-day coaching programme between February and March 2006.

Community leaders and practitioners (such as community cohesion officers) were invited to participate in the project. By the end of the project, about 20 participants were trained in the community narrative approach and were ready to apply their acquired new knowledge and skills to their own context. As part of their training, each participant applied their learnt approach at a community gathering within their local setting. My role as the coach trainer was to facilitate the successful transfer of knowledge in narrative community approaches, and supervise community group practice. The stories shared during those gatherings were collected and prepared for publication (subject to the participants' permission and observing the ethical code such as anonymity and confidentiality).

Over 40 participants attended the community conference which took place toward the end of the project, facilitating further learning, exchange of information and the development of best practice in celebration of their achievement.

Reflection

The purpose of storytelling was to highlight the specific needs of the participants: some of them are highly skilled but face major barriers to finding any employment (skilled or otherwise); or are from the vulnerable groups such as asylum seekers; or are unaccompanied minors. It also aims to develop best practice in helping them to integrate to the host countries; and facilitate the exchange of information between stakeholders (such as non-governmental organizations and the local authorities). It was hoped that a community network could be developed within a conference in the form of telling and re-telling the participants' stories; thus definitional ceremony was used. The conference became a pace setter for the Black History Month which followed.

Many concerns and problems were identified. These included social support language and cultural barriers, and how to access funding to maintain a sustainable community. A number of key themes were developed and an action plan was put forward on how to further develop a community network. In mapping the landscape of the positive action onto the landscape of community consciousness, there was a strong sense of pride, respect;, reassurance, self-awareness and self-realization. It was a pleasant surprise for me to see the 'camp fire' in Karos and Kambro as a metaphor, transported to Peterborough. As a result, the Community Network was formed, and initiated another community gathering supported by the Wildlife Trust in conjunction with the Celebration of the Black History Month which attracted over 200 local people.

There were challenges in the process such as organizing an outdoor event; these included overcoming the rules and regulations of the local authorities in terms of the logistics of holding these events, as well as predicting the changing weather! I was also mindful about my role as a narrative coach – as an ethnographer, it was my responsibility to disseminate the stories of individuals and groups in confidence while at the same time ensuring that due respect was given in honouring those participants who contributed to the stories; as well as providing acknowledgements to all the stakeholders.

Exercise 9.6 Community coaching

Have you had any experience in coaching for diverse communities?

What difficulties and challenges did you encounter?

How did you overcome them?

What approaches did you use?

If you were asked to deliver another coaching programme for your local community, what would you do?

____

____

____

____

Case Study 5 Community Coaching Café

The project – the Community Coaching Café (CCC) – aimed to share the knowledge, skills and experience amongst the local community leaders, entrepreneurs, volunteers and groups in a market town called St Neots, in the UK. My role was as peer to the director of the company (a community interest company) to offer peer supervision at the local coaching psychologist's peer practice group (for further information, see Shams and Law, 2012).

The process

More than 20 volunteers (75 per cent female, 60 per cent over 50, 85 per cent white, 5 per cent South American, 10 per cent black or mixed race, 12 per cent with disability) were provided with 10 hours of coaching training over two days, covering a range of coaching techniques and counselling principles with ongoing supervision. The trained volunteers were matched with suitable coachees. Some of the coaching conversations took place at local spaces such as coffee shops, bars and parks.

Exercise 9.7 Community Coaching Café

What difficulties and challenges do you think such a community coaching programme would face?

What would the issues be for the coaching conversations that take place in public places?

How would you overcome these issues?

____

____

____

____

Reflection

From participating in this project, we have learnt that:

- The local community services have been strengthened through volunteering.
- Learning opportunities may be provided through creative and diverse means.
- Coaching skills are valued in leveraging the mentoring capacity within the local community.
- Sometimes coaching may be embedded in offering guidance including signposting, providing specific advice and factual information.
- Reflection is a core part of learning.
- For some valuable groups, coaching support may be ongoing.
- Like counselling, a coaching conversation provides a social space for many isolated individuals who need the social contact.
- Coaching can help people to improve their skills, confidence, and thereby help the community to flourish.

Exercise 9.8 The quality of a coordinator for community coaching

What qualities, including attributes, knowledge and skills, do you think a coordinator for such a community project would need?

____

____

____

____

Where and how would one acquire the knowledge and skills for making a successful social enterprise?

____

____

____

____

- Both coaches and coachees enjoyed the coaching experience, which provided them with points of entry to take actions, learn experientially and share the learning experience.

An action plan was developed which aimed to:

1. Share the learning with the wider communities.
2. Apply for further funding for developing a community well-being service.
3. Develop a volunteer management consultancy for the third sector.

Evaluation

The evaluation of the CCC project showed an increase in the awareness of the community project; and the stakeholders including the funders were satisfied with the achievements of the volunteers. As a result, the company gained further funding for future projects.

Coaching or Counselling? A Case Study

This section provides you with an additional case study to consider one of the common coaching dilemmas that many of my students and peers have encountered. This particular case was provided by one of my peers from the Community Coaching Café. It illustrates the typical challenges in coaching, especially for those who engage in coaching during the initial stage of their coaching journey.

Carl (a fictitious name), an articulate man, attended a writers group locally. In his first week, he was asked to write about something that meant a lot to him. He chose to write graphically about his attempted suicide, which was so alarming to the group leader that she referred him to me before providing any authoring support to him. Carl had a long history of clinical depression and was receiving treatment from the local mental health charity, part of which was a recovery plan requiring him to accept responsibility for past behaviours. He still periodically feels suicidal though he says he will not act on the feelings now. His preferred style of self-management was to write about his emotional roller-coaster existence as he finds it to be cathartic.

During the initial telephone conversation, he volunteered to present his self-harming experience as an item for the coaching group discussion. He was, at that stage, trying to rebalance himself emotionally to cope with the effects of the medication he was now taking, and was very willing to talk to the coach, and to be offered a one-to-one talk with a suitably experienced coach.

Exercise 9.9

If you were the group leader, what would you do? How would you respond to the situation?

If you were the coach, what would you do? How would you respond to the group's leader's referral?

___

___

___

___

Within the team, the coach felt that she had two options: (i) approach a mental health worker from a national charity who runs CBT classes for men suffering from depression (but who was unavailable at the time); and (ii) invite a very experienced, domestic violence helpline adviser, to offer support.

Carl's aim for the coaching session was to talk about his depression and loss, to get some ideas about how to proceed. Carl said his life at that time was 'out of control'. He had restarted medication for a bipolar condition; he was not sleeping or eating well, and he was distraught that his partner had left home, taking their son with her, and not knowing where they had gone. The sessions were spent exploring the options before him to be able to regain access to his son, and the steps he would need to take to manage himself sufficiently well to present as a positive influence on his son.

The coach encouraged him to examine what specifically had led to this situation; to recall instances when he had managed himself and his relationships better; encouraged him that he could do so again; helped him reframe his situation by viewing it from his partner's and son's perspectives; and created a very personal action plan so he could be in a better position to take advantage of any opportunity which arose, to rebuild his relationship with his son. This addressed various self-management challenges that required a change of behaviour, which initially he seemed overwhelmed by, but which, by the end of the second session, he was motivated to try. The coach forwarded him information about access rights by email. According to Carl's feedback, he felt he now had a way forward. He rated the coach as

Exercise 9.10

How would you assess the above situation?

How would you evaluate this coaching session?

How would you view the coaching session from your code of ethics?

If you were the peer supervisor to the coach, what would you say to her?

Refer to your code of ethics – which ethical principle would be applicable here?

____

____

____

____

'100 per cent effective, the coffee shop setting as suitable, and thought his aims had been partially achieved'.

From the above case study, we can see that coaching in the real world can be very challenging; sometimes it may be difficult to draw a line between coaching and counselling. For further discussion, see Buckley and Buckley (2006).

Chapter Summary and Reflection

This chapter has shown you examples of how coaching has been applied in the real world. You will probably have noted the complexity of each case – the multiple stakeholders and multi-layered narratives, in different organizations and contexts. Having read though these case studies and completed the related exercises, I hope you have learnt how to do reflection-in-action; and that you are ready to develop a portfolio of case studies by writing your own reflective logs. Using the framework as discussed in this chapter and the template in the Appendix will help you along the way.

10

Evaluation and Evidence-based Coaching

Why is it important? And how to ...

Introduction

The coaching literature usually offers illustrations of different techniques. Evaluation is an important part of the coaching process and yet the most neglected area in practice. To improve the success of coaching and its acceptance by mainstream psychology as a serious discipline, formal evaluation is a prerequisite. This involves more than simply asking the coachee at the end of the session, as many coaches would do, 'How do you feel?'

While a formal evaluation methodology has been established, usually this is only used for large-scale evaluation, rather than for coaching or coaching practice. Nevertheless evidence-based evaluation has been vigorously applied to clinical practice (such as medicine and clinical psychological intervention). No formal protocol has so far been established for coaching practice. This has become one of the major critiques of both coaching and coaching psychology. Coaching, especially coaching psychology, is increasingly regarding evaluation as a formal part of the intervention. At the time of writing, any formal evaluation of coaching still remains relatively rare, and is regarded as a minority practice. Urgent action needs to be taken by the coaching community and individual practitioners if coaching is to continue to flourish.

As emphasized throughout this book, there is a clear need for evidence-based evaluation on the effectiveness of coaching and coaching applications. I propose in this chapter that the evaluation of coaching depends on

Coaching Psychology: A Practitioner's Guide, First Edition. Ho Law.

the levels of analyses. The key question is: *Are the evaluation methods appropriate? To whom? In what context? For what purpose?*

Exercise 10.1

What is meant by 'evidence in coaching'?

____

____

____

____

By evidence, I mean:

- the application of well-established psychological theories or coaching models in your practice; or
- evaluation of the effectiveness of your practice.

This chapter summarizes the evaluation methodology, tools and techniques for coaching and mentoring programmes. It provides a step-by-step evaluation framework for you to evaluate your own coaching practice.

I shall first discuss the different levels of evaluation and then provide some detail about evaluation methodology. This links to the context of coaching in terms of its model development, design, application and training.

Levels of Evaluation

As many coaching practitioners and coaches know, there are different scales in terms of coaching programmes and therefore of evaluations. These could range from a single session to several months (sometimes for large-scale organizational change programmes, they may well run for more than a year). Depending on the context, evaluation may consist of the following levels:

1. individual
2. group
3. organization
4. society.

Exercise 10.2

How would you evaluate your own coaching practice in terms of:

1. individual
2. group
3. organization
4. society?

The effectiveness of your coaching practice can be evaluated in two ways:

- By comparing the condition at the beginning and at the end of the coaching journey.
- By comparing between those who take the coaching journey and those who do not.

A popular model for evaluation, developed by Kirkpatrick (1959), has been used in training. This may also be relevant to coaching applications. The model also consists of four levels:

1. reaction to the programme and planned action
2. learning
3. behavioural change
4. business results.

At the *individual* level, coaches and coaching practitioners would very often collect feedback from the coachee. This could range from an elaborate feedback form with a five-point Likert-type scale to individual questions and informal questioning at the end of a session or programme. This would only capture level 1 of Kirkpatrick's model, which is the coachee's emotional reaction to the intervention. However, it does not enable the coach to learn from the practice (level 2) and evaluate the possible coaching outcome – which very often is about behavioural change (level 3). While a coaching programme for organizations would usually require evaluation of the business results such as return on investment (ROI), I would argue that even for individuals, it is important for coaches to demonstrate that their intervention provides value for money. Even if the coaching were provided for free, it would still be important that it can justify the time and other resources required (level 4). Thus we recommend that coaches and coaching psychology practitioners should consider evaluation of their practice that covers all four levels of the Kirkpatrick model, irrespective of whether it is for individuals or organizations. Obviously, it would not be cost-effective to carry out a formal evaluation for a single session. In this case, I suggest that coaches should still aim to use well-tested coaching techniques and collect individual feedback as part of the ongoing evaluation of their coaching effectiveness.

For *group* coaching, the same principles as discussed above should apply. This would generate a large set of data for evaluation. A group with N participants would generate N sets of data about a coaching session. Thus a more detailed design on questionnaire and methodology may be worthwhile (for example, Law and FitzGerald, 2012).

Large-Scale Evaluation

The *organizational* level usually involves the coaching buyer (e.g. HR manager) raising a purchase order. A large coaching programme would likely require a large-scale evaluation, very often as part of the tendering requirement and coaching contract from the outset. From the coaching buyer's perspective, evaluation is only part of a larger framework. For the public sector in the UK, the Department of Trade & Industry (2006), in accordance with HM Treasury's *Green Book* guidance (HMSO, 1997), recommended the ROAMEF Framework. This consists of the following components (see Figure 10.1):

1. Rationale
2. Objectives
3. Appraisal
4. Monitoring
5. Evaluation
6. Feedback.

Step 1: Rationale

According to the ROAMEF Framework, as a first step, before any consideration about purchasing a coaching programme, it is necessary to have a rationale behind the intention. The rationale consists of two things: *needs*

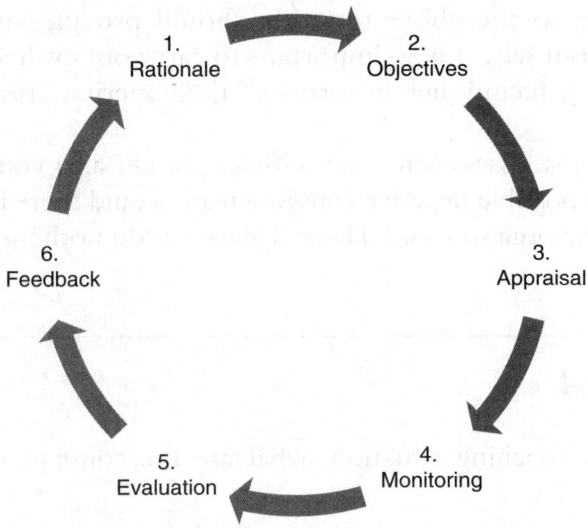

Figure 10.1 Integrated ROAMEF Framework. Source: Adopted from http://www.hm-treasury.gov.uk/d/green_book_complete.pdf

and *benefits*. For an organization, the needs are very often considered from the organizational perspective rather than the individual employees (coachees) themselves. The benefit of the proposed coaching programme has to be greater than its cost and outweigh the risk. Both the needs and benefits have to be identified so that a business case can be made.

From the rationale, a number of options can be generated. There may be alternative solutions to coaching intervention. Even within the coaching option, there are a number of possible competing proposals in terms of coaching techniques, for example CBT, GROW model, and so on.

Exercise 10.3

Which coaching technique should be adopted for your own coaching programme?

____

____

____

____

The answers to the above question should provide you with some indications about why it is so important to carry out evaluation for individual coaching techniques in terms of their merits, effectiveness and efficiency.

In terms of risk assessment, the initiator should also consider a list of implications of possible negative consequences: would there be any adverse impact upon the organization? There is always a 'do nothing option'.

Exercise 10.4

Think about a coaching situation, what are the consequences of doing nothing?

____

____

____

____

Step 2: Objectives

The second step is to describe the objectives of the proposed coaching programme. This sets out *what* the intervention is intended to achieve rather than *how* it can be achieved. The question of whether to buy into coaching or CBT coaching, for example, should not come into the discussion at this stage.

Step 3: Appraisal

This step is the most significant part of making a business case for the proposal. As suggested earlier, there are likely to be many competing options (including the 'do nothing' option) to be considered; all of them may claim that they can meet the objectives identified. The do nothing option should act as a baseline to measure against the selected options. An econometric technique known as cost-benefit analysis (CBA) is usually used in the private sector; in the public sector, especially for applications that are about quality of life rather than profit, cost-effectiveness analysis (CEA) is used instead. Both cases require the cost of the intervention to be quantified, for example, 'Programme X would cost £15k over 12 months, as a result, 200 managers would be trained with the coaching technique that would enable them to manage the change programme better'. In this example, *how* managers manage change better is yet to be specified.

Step 4: Monitoring

Once a coaching programme has been successfully appraised, its progress should be continuously monitored to ensure that it is being implemented according to the plan. For a coaching programme, it is useful to ask the coachees to keep a journal to describe their learning and experience. This would not only allow them to reflect on what is learnt but also enable the manager and the coach to monitor their development. The information may also be useful for evaluation at the next stage.

Step 5: Evaluation

The primary purpose of evaluation concerns the objectives:

- Have the objectives been met?
- To what extent have they been met?

Both the coach and coachees should also evaluate their learning:

- What lessons have I learnt from the coaching programme?
- Were there any unexpected surprises during the programme?
- What will I do differently in the future?

The above would form part of the ongoing professional development. For the coach, this is very important for the refinement of future coaching practice.

In terms of formal methodology, there are two types of evaluation (Law, Ireland and Hussain, 2007):

- process evaluation
- impact evaluation.

The two approaches complement each other (see Figure 10.2).

Process evaluation

Process evaluation aims to analyse the process of the coaching at the implementation phase and to evaluate any successes and failures of the coaching activities involved in that process. In order to understand what works, so that the future coaching approach can be improved, the coach should

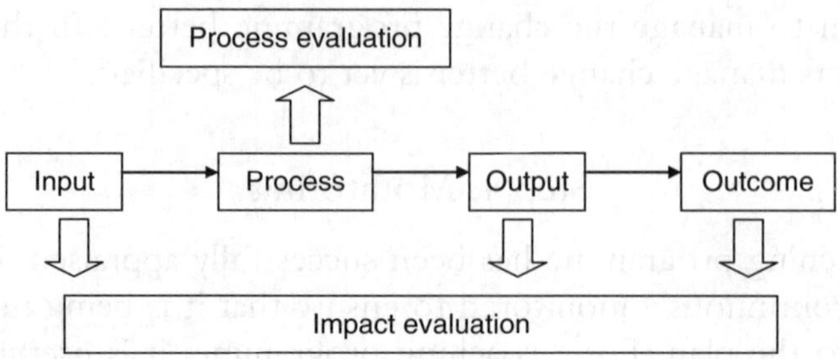

Figure 10.2 Evaluation methodology. Source: Law, Ireland and Hussain, 2007

always carry out a *process* evaluation. This involves collecting information on good practice e.g. any successful story during the coaching process.

Exercise 10.5

Reflect on the case studies that you have collected, either your own or those described in Chapter 9, consider the following question:

Which coaching techniques have contributed most to the coaching outcome?

____

____

____

____

The coach may collect descriptions of the coaching activity from the coachees. This is one of the reasons why it is so important for the coach to maintain the reflective log.

Semi-structured interviews with coachees may also be used to supplement the case studies. The coach may also seek out views from other stakeholders. The data collected would be mostly qualitative.

Impact evaluation

Impact evaluation works backwards; it links the outcome of the coaching programme to its output and input. It is the most vigorous way

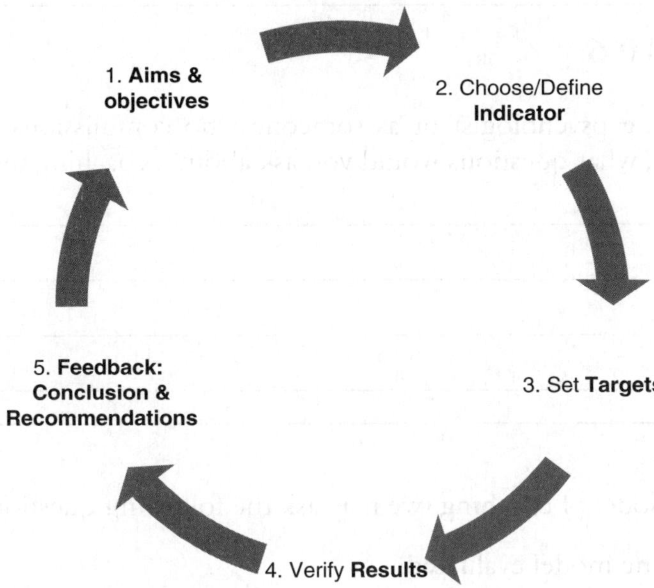

Figure 10.3 Impact evaluation

to assess the extent to which the coaching intervention has met its objectives, as it usually demands evidence-based measures. It is also a powerful tool for demonstrating *value for money* to the stakeholders. The data collected is usually quantitative. Thus statistical analyses can be performed. The key step of impact evaluation is to identify the key performance indicators that link to the coaching aims and objectives (see Figure 10.3).

Quantitative Analysis and Evaluation of Coaching Models

As the previous section shows, formal evaluation is a non-trivial task. The process requires considerable investment in terms of cost and resources. Not many activities or coaching programmes are subjected to a vigorous form of evaluation, which is required not only for the organization's commissioning but also for the long-term research and development of a discipline.

As a discipline, coaching psychology is relatively in its infancy in terms of its development. Thus more cases of formal evaluation are required at each stage of its development, that is, developing a model of coaching, coaching design, application and training.

Exercise 10.6

As a coaching psychologist or as someone who commissions a coaching programme, what questions would you ask about a coaching model?

____

____

____

____

On the model of coaching, we may ask the following questions:

- How is the model evaluated?
- How do we know that it works?
- What are the key factors?
- How do the key factors affect the outcome?

One argument against any possible vigorous quantitative analyses has been the fact that, by definition, coaching is about conversations between individuals; and many of the coachees are usually high performers. Each individual is a single case (with all the human idiosyncrasies), thus the use of statistical analysis for evaluation has been attacked by many coaching practitioners as inappropriate. A typical example cited for the argument would be: given say 100 performers ($N = 100$), the statistics would only show the mean and provide the characteristic of the average performer. Or, if probability $p = 0.5$, how do you know if there are two significant patterns rather than no pattern?

This argument reflects the lack of knowledge of the practitioners about statistical evaluation rather than the 'truth'. For the former case, any competent researchers engaging in a large-scale research of high performers would know that they would not mix the high performers with the low performers in their sampling and take an average. They are studying a group of high performers and taking the mean performance of the high performers. Using appropriate statistical techniques such as factor analyses, certain significant factors that are common to many high performers could be identified (e.g. high cognitive capacity, quick to learn, long retention span). An average performance (from a group of high performers) would be significantly higher than the average performance of a mixed group of performers. The keys are in 'design' and 'control' of the evaluation.

For the latter case ($p = 0.5$), once again, people who have learnt how to do statistical analyses properly would know that you do not simply look at the value of probability. Before you even attempt to use the statistical test, you would first examine the data set and its pattern – do a scatterplot. If there are two significant patterns appearing in the sample, a 'binomial' distribution would not escape the trained eye. To draw any single inference from the statistical test, it should have satisfied a number of conditions: a 'normal' distribution is one. The solution to such an observation is simply to separate the two samples and choose appropriate statistical tests accordingly.

Like any scientific discipline, there are no empirical issues in the study of coaching. The issue is a matter of personal preference. So far most the coaching models are descriptive such as GROW and UIF/ILS (Law, 2013). Furthermore, for coaching applications, there is no reason why the outcome of the coaching application cannot be subjected to evidence-based impact evaluation.

Research and Evidenced-based Coaching

The evaluation criteria for any coaching model, as proposed by the coaching community, is: *Does it work?*

Translating the above question into practice, a coaching model needs to satisfy two sets of criteria: (i) Can it be learned? (ii) Is the result replicable? In other words, having learned the model, can another coach produce the same results as the expert coach who used the model?

However, the specific criteria for (i) learning and (ii) repeatability have been only vaguely defined, and are a subject for further research. This has important implications to model refinement and the development of new models of coaching. So far this process is very much craft-based, depending on the ingenuity and intuition of the coach who works on a trial-and-error basis. For instance NLP coaching models were refined by Bandler and Grinder who systematically tested each step of the code to see whether the models could produce the same result if that step was missing. In doing so, they successfully eliminated some of the human idiosyncrasy of the model. Thus the resulting model can be generic.

From the research point of view, the above process is painstaking and extremely inefficient. What if there are thousands of variables in a coaching model (and a programme may use many different coaching models and techniques)? The resulting coaching model in practice is likely to be complex. Using the trial-and-error method would be virtually impossible. This places quite an obstacle to the progress of coaching development as a scientific discipline.

A large-scale research programme with a larger pool of participants using vigorous quantitative analyses may offer a more efficient solution. This would also make formal evaluation possible. Furthermore, if the models developed were theory-based (guided by established psychological principles), they are more likely to show which coaching models are idiosyncratic. By combining the theory and vigorous evaluation methodology, the coaching model generated in this way would more likely be evidence based and produce a greater impact upon the individuals and organizations than the current state of art can offer. As Palmer (2007: xi) pointed out, 'Applying evidence-based practice is the challenge facing the profession of coaching and mentoring, as we need more research to inform our practice.'

Indeed, evidence-based coaching has become the 'lofty standard' that coaches aspire to adopt in their practice. Many coaches, especially NLP coaches, argue that coaching is an art and as such it may not be appropriate to use experimental design for its evaluation. Furthermore, coaching (especially in leadership coaching) is often about coaching a 'high achiever' who is usually exceptional (rather than representative). However, this is not always the case (as shown in Chapter 9). Even the NLP (its second model: representational model) was developed based on the observation of groups of people rather than modelling a particular individual. (Those people were in the gestalt therapy group, not geniuses either, though this is not my point of argument here.) I would argue that with a careful evaluation design and suitable statistical methods, both formal and informal coaching models can be achieved.

Applying evaluation strategy to individual coaching

Exercise 10.7

If you only have one coachee, how would you apply the formal evaluation strategy described earlier to the individual coaching sessions?

____

____

____

____

Most coaching practice so far has been in one-to-one coaching (or group training). For many coaching practitioners, the relevant question on evaluation may be, 'Can the formal evaluation strategy described earlier be applied to individual coaching sessions?' As indicated, this is possible and indeed recommended. Indeed, we can argue that the coaching practice is well formed for such evaluative practice. For instance, the key component in impact evaluation is the *outcome* of the programme. At an individual level, a coaching question about coaching also concerns a well-formed outcome.

The 'outcome' component is regarded as a fundamental feature of the coaching practice. In coaching, outcomes need to be 'well formed' (e.g. SMARTER objectives). When defining an outcome, you may find the following questions useful as a checklist:

- Is it in the positive? What do you want? What is the pay-off? How does that help you?
- Does the individual have ownership of the goal? How will you make this happen? What will you do? What if he/she doesn't agree?
- Is it specific? How will you know when you achieve this goal? What are the performance criteria? How will you test the criteria?
- Do you really want to achieve this goal?
- Who says you have to do this? How will this help you? So what?
- Does the outcome preserve the byproduct of the current behaviour? What positive things do you get from your present way of achieving goals? In what way will these be preserved in achieving your new goal? Are there any positive things which need to be put to one side to achieve the goal? Are there any new things which need to be incorporated so as to achieve this goal? How will you achieve this incorporation?
- Is the outcome ecological? Are there any times you would not do this? Does any part of you object to doing this in this context?
- When will you achieve this goal? Will you achieve all of the goal then, or just a part of it?

It is therefore concluded that the evaluation outcome and coaching outcome should be linked. This would ensure that the coachee's outcome is well formed and that coaches can continue to collect data to improve their coaching practice.

Step 6: Feedback

Having completed the evaluation, you should provide feedback to your clients and coachees. These may be in different forms – verbal and/or written reports. This may be formal or informal, depending on the nature and size of the project.

Exercise 10.8

How would you provide feedback to your coachee individually, or to the customer who sponsored the coaching project for an organization?

____

____

____

____

Chapter Summary

In this chapter, you have learnt about a formal evaluation framework in terms of process and impact evolution. It has shown how this framework may be applied to different levels: individual, group and organzation. There is a higher level of evaluation, that is at the level of society. However, this is beyond the scope of this chapter. I have also advocated a vigorous research programme on development and evaluation of coaching model and applications using both qualitative as well as quantitative approaches. The latter has been a relatively neglected area within the coaching development. Coaches and coaching buyers should:

- Establish a formal evaluation process as part of the coaching programme.
- Develop an evaluation strategy that is fit for purpose.
- Discuss evaluation methodology with sponsors, clients and coachees at the outset.
- Conduct ongoing research and development about the coaching modelling and applications.
- Maintain a coaching log for future learning and evaluation.

11

Reflection and Resources

Where can I get further training, support and information?

So now you have almost finished reading this book; and probably practised many of the exercises in coaching psychology. In this concluding chapter, I invite you to consider the implications of undertaking continuous professional development and, if necessary, further training. The end of the book marks a significant juncture in your coaching journey. It provides you a rite of passage to becoming a professional – someone who is an experienced practitioner in a particular discipline. You may like to reflect on this and its meaning – what does it mean to be a professional?

Personal Reflection

Coaching psychology as a profession has travelled a long way. In the UK, since the formation of the Special Group in Coaching Psychology (SGCP) within the British Psychological Society (BPS) in 2004, a Register of Coaching Psychologists was finally set up in 2012. It signifies the Society's recognition for those who have specialist expertise in the field of coaching psychology. It also provides a key resource for the public, especially the coaching buyers who wish to access the services of coaching psychology.

Applicants for the Register are required to confirm that they:

1. Have knowledge of the contexts (including professional, ethical and legal) within which coaching psychology is provided.

Coaching Psychology: A Practitioner's Guide, First Edition. Ho Law.

2. Understand the responsibility and limitations of the professional role, including maintaining boundaries, confidentiality and accountability.
3. Understand issues pertaining to difference and diversity in coaching psychology.
4. Can address ethical issues in coaching psychology and understand how these may affect the coaching process, including power differentials.
5. Understand what is meant by a safe environment in practising coaching psychology and the factors that affect the development of a coaching relationship.
6. Have knowledge and experience of different coaching and coaching psychology frameworks, orientations and methods.
7. Have skills and experience in contracting and negotiating with clients.
8. Have skills and experience in establishing, developing and maintaining a coaching relationship.
9. Have knowledge of the structure of professional coaching psychology experience including assessment procedures, interventions and the changing expectations regarding the practitioner's role.
10. Have knowledge of theories of management and other specialisms relevant to the application of coaching psychology.
11. Have knowledge of the various mediums for providing psychological coaching (self-report, psychometrics, CDs, colleague reports and appraisals).
12. Have knowledge of techniques and processes to evaluate coaching psychology, including receiving feedback from the clients on their perceptions of progress and their expectations of outcomes of coaching psychology.
13. Maintain up-to-date awareness of the development of coaching psychology theory and practice and engage in coaching psychology CPD (BPS, 2012).

At present, the Register is open to Chartered Psychologists who are also members of the SGCP only. However, it is envisaged that training routes offering individuals to become a Registered Coaching Psychologist will follow soon.

Those who have travelled with me along the route of this professional development know that the journey has been far from easy. To champion the diverse opinions of stakeholders about what the new profession should be, and transform these views into collective action, is no easy task. However, throughout this journey, we are clear about the importance of developing and holding onto our ethical values and principles. The coaching psychology, as a new profession, in common with those of other psychological disciplines, is about being human; it is about helping people, helping them to achieve their aspirations, hopes and dreams; it is about overcoming the obstacles along the way (be they environmental, cultural, social or psychological) – it is grounded in our lived experience. It is a privileged profession through which we can share those lived experiences.

The above does highlight the additional requirement of the profession. The BPS Register requires coaching psychologists to receive ongoing supervision for their coaching psychology practice from a supervisor who is a qualified psychologist (i.e. either a Chartered Psychologist or registered with the Health Professions Council in the UK). Other countries may have different or similar requirements. This is because, apart from having the coaching knowledge and skill, coaching requires us to engage with other human beings ethically. And as we know, owing to the complexity of the coaching context, maintaining an appropriate professional role in engaging with coachees is sometimes challenging. A coaching relationship is different from other relationships (personal, counselling or therapeutic) in that it requires one to maintain the professional boundaries between multiple stakeholders (Law, 2006). With ongoing supervision and CPD, writing and keeping a reflective log will also help. The benefits of both supervision and CPD are that they help you to:

1. Increase your awareness about your experience (what you have done in the coaching session).
2. Learn from the practice.
3. Develop conceptual knowledge and further refine your model of coaching.
4. Integrate your learning into future practice.
5. Improve your skills to overcome future challenges.
6. Monitor your progress.
7. Maintain balance and well-being.

Throughout this book, I have emphasized learning as a foundation in coaching practice. Also, as I argued in Chapter 10, I believe an 'evidence-based' model of coaching and psychology has much to offer in providing a wealth of established theories and principles. It is important for the future of our profession that we continue to do research and develop a foundation for evidence-based practice. Although this book may have already satisfied your initial curiosity, you may want to further advance your development.

Here and now, this moment also marks a significant juncture of your coaching journey – in terms of its transition to the future, which in the coaching sense, is open to change. Looking ahead, it is now up to you to choose which direction to travel, continue to search, research, learn and develop. To help you to start the next journey and along the way, the rest of this chapter provides some relevant sources of information for further training and reading. Good luck and enjoy the journey!

Academic Institutions, Professional Societies and Government Body

Organizations that offer further training or professional support in coaching psychology are grouped into the following categories:

- academic institutions
- professional societies for psychology and coaching psychology
- government body for regulating registered psychologists.

These are listed in the sections below. As you will notice, at present, there are only two universities in the UK and one in Ireland that provide coaching psychology as an academic discipline. There are some other institutions which may have embedded coaching psychology in their core programmes (such as psychology or coaching qualifications) which are not included here.

Academic institutions

School of Psychology,
University of East London (UEL)
Stratford Campus
Water Lane
London
E15 4LZ

http://www.uel.ac.uk/postgraduate/specs/coachingpsychology-dl/

The School of Psychology at UEL offers postgraduate options in coaching psychology for students with appropriate undergraduate degrees and/or substantial work experience. The Coaching Psychology Programme consists of Post Graduate Certificate, Post Graduate Diploma and MSc courses and the UEL also offers a broad range of coaching services, including:

- short courses for managers
- specialist short courses for professional coaches
- coaching supervision
- postgraduate training in coaching psychology

- coaching research
- coaching evaluation.

City University London
Northampton Square
London
EC1V 0HB

http://www.city.ac.uk/psychology/research/CoachPsych/CoachPsych.html

The Coaching Psychology Unit at City University was launched on 19 December 2005. It was the first university-based coaching psychology unit in the UK. It offers PhD programmes for qualified psychologists (e.g. Chartered or Registered Psychologists in the UK). It focuses on research into all aspects of the developing field of coaching psychology and coaching. This includes:

- developing the theory and practice of coaching psychology
- effectiveness of coaching and coaching psychology practice
- return on investment of coaching in organizations
- leadership development through coaching
- the adaptation of therapeutic approaches to the field of coaching
- boundaries between coaching, coaching psychology, mentoring, counselling and psychotherapy
- coaching in multicultural settings, organizations and society
- coaching to reduce stress and enhance performance
- internet coaching interventions
- health coaching and well-being
- positive psychology and coaching psychology.

School of Applied Psychology
University College Cork
Enterprise Centre
North Mall
Cork
Ireland

www.ucc.ie/en/apsych/

In Ireland, along with the currently taught postgraduate programmes, the School of Applied Psychology, from September 2013 and subject to final confirmation, will introduce an MA in Coaching Psychology for those with graduate basis for registration, along with an MA in Coaching for non-psychologists. Links for these new courses will be available in due course from the main link above.

Professional societies for psychology and coaching psychology

The British Psychological Society (BPS)
St Andrews House
48 Princess Road East
Leicester
LE1 7DR
Tel: +44 (0)116 254 9568
Fax: +44 (0)116 227 1314
E-mail: enquiries@bps.org.uk
http://www.bps.org.uk/

Due to the popularity of coaching, increasingly there are a number of qualified psychologists who have acquired the skills and knowledge of coaching psychology as part of their CPD; they would also be reliable providers if they offer coaching and/or training. For instance the British Psychological Society required its Chartered members to have postgraduate qualifications (such as doctorate or MSc) plus post qualification supervised by Chartered Psychologists. This implies that the duration of training is about five years (including their first degree in psychology which usually takes three years). Many of these psychologists are state registered and regulated by the Health Professions Council under the new legislation in 2009. Thus the title to look out for with qualified psychologists who offer coaching and training would be 'Registered Psychologist' and/or 'Chartered Psychologist'.

International Society for Coaching Psychology
http://www.isfcp.net/

Internationally, the new International Society for Coaching Psychology (which was founded in 2008) requires psychologists who are qualified in their own country (for example 'Registered Psychologists' and/or 'Chartered Psychologists' in the UK) and to become full members they have to demonstrate their competence in terms of a minimum of 80 hours in coaching psychology as part of their CPD over two years.

Government body for regulating registered psychologists

The Health Professions Council (HPC) is a regulator in the UK. It was set up to protect the public. To do this, it keeps a register of health professionals who meet its standards for their training, professional skills, behaviour and health. At the time of writing, over 200,000 professionals from 16 professions were registered. Since 1 July 2009, practitioner psychologists became the fourteenth profession to be regulated by the HPC. Although, at present, coaches and coaching psychologists are not being regulated by the HPC (or any other government body in the UK), it may still be useful to know if the psychologists who are practising coaching are on the register (especially for those who seek coaching services or supervision). On 1 August 2012 the HPC changed its name to the Health and Care Professions Council (HCPC). This decision was made by the government and by the Health and Social Care Act 2012, which will empower it to take on the regulation of social workers in England. As not everyone registered with the HCPC works in 'health' or 'care', the name was chosen to better describe the diverse range of professions it regulates.

Each of the 16 professions has at least one professional title that is protected by law. For psychologists, these include 'Practitioner Psychologist' and 'Registered Psychologist' and various other adjective titles. This means that anyone using these protected titles must be registered with the HCPC – it is a criminal offence for someone to claim that they are registered (qualified) when they are not, or to use a protected title that they are not entitled to. The HPC will prosecute people who commit these crimes.

If a health professional does not meet its standards, the HCPC can take action which might include stopping the individuals concerned from practising. This means that if you are unhappy with treatment you are given, or worried about the behaviour or health of a registered psychologist, you can always raise your concerns with the HCPC. The HCPC aims to protect the public and ensures that it always provides the best quality of service for all its stakeholders with a Quality Management System (BSI to ISO 9001:2008) in place. Further information can be found here:

Health and Care Professions Council (HCPC)
Park House
184 Kennington Park Road
London
SE11 4BU
Tel : +44 (0) 20 7582 0866
http://www.hcpc-uk.org/

As mentioned earlier, the protected title to look out for with qualified psychologists (whether they offer coaching, training or any other services) in the UK would be 'Registered Psychologist'. You can check whether a specified person is a Registered Psychologist by visiting the web site below:

http://www.hcpc-uk.org/check/

As part of the grand parenting process to set up the register, all the qualified practitioner psychologists who are Chartered Psychologists (previously on the BPS register) were transferred onto the HPC (now HCPC) register. However, the BPS still maintains a directory for its members who are 'Chartered Psychologist', though the nature and implication of such a title would be very different (i.e. possibly become just a category of membership). You may still check whether a specified person is a Chartered Psychologist via the following web site:

http://www.bps.org.uk/bps/e-services/find-a-psychologist/register.cfm

Different countries will have different legislation and systems of regulating psychological practice. For instance, Australia has Psychologists Registration Boards (similar to the HCPC) for different geographical regions (e.g. West Australia). You are advised to check the regulations in your own country.

Appendix: Writing Your Own Reflective Log

Step 1: Description – identify a significant event; describe what happened (focus on the concrete experience).

1.1 Introduction – provide a brief description of the context of the event and the background including stakeholders.

1.2 Summary of the process – succinctly describe the process; stating what you did and why.

Coaching Psychology: A Practitioner's Guide, First Edition. Ho Law.

Step 2: Cognition and emotion – reflect on your thoughts and feelings. What were you thinking/feeling during the engagement? (If it was a coaching/mentoring session, what do you think about the coachee's thoughts and feelings?)

2.1 Mood (Describe the emotion. How did you feel? How did your coachee feel?)

2.2 Thought (What was going through your mind? What was your coachee thinking about?)

Step 3: Analysis – try to understand what happened and draw meaning from the experience.

Reflection 1: What sense can you make of the experience? How well do you think the process has been delivered? What went well and what did not go so well? How do you understand the beliefs, values and experiences of your coachee/mentee, yourself? How have these self-values and concepts impacted on them during these interactions, how were these understood and managed, and how did they transform the coaching outcome?

Step 4: Evaluation – assess the intended and unintended consequences of the experience

Reflection 2: From Reflection 1, would you have done anything differently? What else could you have done? What have you learnt and what would you do differently in the future?

Step 5: Conclusion – summarize the meaning and lessons learned; look for improvement.

Reflection 3: On balance, what is your conclusion? What have you learnt?

Step 6: Action plan – recommend a future plan of action for further learning and improvement. If a similar situation arose again, what would you do? What are you going to do to further improve and develop yourself/ your performance?

Provide a personal development plan as a result of the above learning.

And finally…

Mood now – having achieved the above, how do you feel NOW?

References

Alexander, G. (2006) Behavioural coaching: The GROW model, in *Excellence in Coaching – Industry Guide* (ed. J. Passmore), Kogan Page, London, pp. 61–72.

Alimo-Metcalfe, B. and Pritchett, P. (2008) Coaching for transformational leadership: ELQ, in *Psychometrics in Coaching* (ed. J. Passmore), Kogan Page, London.

Allan, J. and Law, H. (2009) Ethical navigation in coaching psychology – a Socratic dialogue. *The Coaching Psychologist*, 5 (2), 115–126.

Alli, A. (1977) Orientation – principles, techniques, and philosophy of a ritual technology for self-initiation, http://www.paratheatrical.com (accessed 4 August 2012).

Alli, A. (2003) *Towards an Archaeology of the Soul*, Vertical Pool Publishing, California.

Allport, G.W. (1954) *The Nature of Prejudice*, Addison-Wesley, Reading, MA.

Allport, G.W. (1961) *Pattern and Growth in Personality*, Holt, Rinehart & Winston, New York.

Anderson, A.G. and Ceicil, S. (2006) Reflection on Athens. *Sport and Exercise Psychology Review*, 2 (2).

Anderson, A.G., Knowles, Z. and Gilbourne, D. (2004) Reflective practice for sport psychologists: concepts, models, practical implications on dissemination. *The Sport Psychologist*, 18, 188–203.

Anderson, R.C., Spiro, R.J. and Anderson, M.C. (1978) Schemata as scaffolding for the representation of information in connected discourse. *American Educational Research Journal*, 15, 433–440.

Coaching Psychology: A Practitioner's Guide, First Edition. Ho Law.

Aquilina, R. and Law, H.C. (2012) An executive coaching program to support nurse managers achieve organizational objectives – an action research. Conference Proceedings for the AMON 3rd International Orthopaedic Nursing Conference, 11–12 October, Qawra, Malta.

Argyris, C. (1977) Double loop learning in organisations. *Harvard Business Review*, 55 (5), 115–125.

Argyris, C. (1999) *On Organisational Learning*, 2nd edn, Blackwell, Oxford.

Argyris, C. and Schön, D.A. (1978) *Organisational Learning: A Theory of Action Perspective*, Addison-Wesley, Reading, MA.

Arvedson, L. (1993) Coming to grips with learning organisations. *European Forum for Management*, 1, 5–10.

Association for Coaching (2012) Coaching definitions, http://www.associationfor coaching.com/about/about03.htm (accessed 4 August 2012).

Ausbel, D.P. (1968). *Educational Psychology: A Cognitive View*, Holt, Rinehart and Winston, New York.

Ausbel, D.P. and Fitzgerald, D. (1962) Organizer, general background and antecedent learning variables in sequential verbal learning. *Journal of Educational Psychology*, 53, 243–249.

Ausbel, D.P. and Youssef, M. (1963). The role of discriminability in meaningful parallel learning. *Journal of Educational Psychology*, 54, 331–336.

Baltes, P.B., Reese, H.W. and Lipsitt, L.P. (1980) Life-span developmental psychology. *Annual Review of Psychology*, 31, 65–110.

Bandler, R. and Grinder, J. (1975) *The Structure of Magic I: A Book About Language and Therapy*, Science and Behavior Books, Palo Alto, CA.

Bandura, A. (1977) Self-efficacy: Toward a unifying theory of behavioural change. *Psychological Review*, 84, 195–215.

Bandura, A. (1982) Self-efficacy mechanism in human agency. *American Psychologist*, 37, 122–147.

Bandura, A. (1986) *Social Foundations of Thought And Action: A Social-Cognitive Theory*, Prentice-Hall, Englewood Cliffs, NJ.

Bandura, A. (1997) *Self-efficacy: The Exercise of Control*, W.H. Freeman, New York.

Barchard, K.A. (2003) Does emotional intelligence assist in the prediction of academic success? *Educational and Psychological Measurement*, 63, 840--858.

Bargh, J.A., McKenna, K.Y.A. and Fitzsimons, G.M. (2002) Can you see the real me? Activation and expressions of the 'true self' on the Internet. *Journal of Social Issues*, 58 (1), 33–48.

Barnes, F.P. and Mudin, L. (2001) *Values and Ethics in the Practice of Psychotherapy and Counselling*, Open University Press, Buckingham.

Bartlett, F.C. (1932) *Remembering: A Study in Experimental and Social Psychology*, Cambridge University Press, Cambridge.

Bass, B.M. (1985) *Transformational Leadership: Industrial, Military, and Educational Impact*, Erlbaum, Mahwah, NJ.

Bateson, G. (1972) *Steps to an Ecology of Mind*, Ballantine, New York.

Beck, A., Rush, A., Shaw, B. and Emery, G. (1979) *Cognitive Therapy of Depression*, Guilford Press, New York.

Beisser, A.R. (1970) The paradoxical theory of change, in *Gestalt Therapy Now* (eds J. Fagan and I.L. Shepherd), Palo Alto, CA, pp. 77–80.

Belenky, M.F., Clinchy, B.M., Goldberger, M.R. and Tarule, J.M. (1986) *Woman's Ways of Knowing: The Development of Self, Voice and Mind*, Basic Books, New York.

Bell, J. and Hardiman, R. (1989) The third role – the naturalistic knowledge engineer, in *Knowledge Elicitation – Principles, Technques and Applications* (ed. D. Diaper), Ellis Horwood, Chichester.

Bennet, D.T. (1997) Telementoring young Women in science, engineering and computing, in *Proceedings of the Women in Engineering Conference* (ed. S.S. Metz), Stevenson Institute of Technology, Hoboken, NJ, pp. 271–276.

Blackler, F., Crump, N. and McDonald, S. (1999) Organisational learning and organisational forgetting, in *Organisational Learning and Learning Organisation: Development in Theory and Practice* (eds M. Easterby-Smith, J. Burgoyne and L. Araujo), Sage, London.

Bockler, J. (2006a) Celebrating our story … 100 years of transpersonal psychology. *The Transpersonal Psychology Review*, 10 (1), 119.

Bockler, J. (2006b) Alchemy: Ritual expeditions into the psyche. Presentation at the 10th Annual Conference of Transpersonal Psychology Section, British Psychological Society.

Bor, R. and Legg, C. (2003) The systems paradigm, in *Handbook of Counselling Psychology*, 2nd edn (eds R. Woolfe, W, Dryden and S. Strawbridge), Sage, London.

Bostic St. Clair, C. and Grinder, J. (2001) *Whispering in the Wind*, J&C Enterprises, Scotts Valley, CA.

Boud, D. (1995) *Enhancing Learning Through Self-assessment*, Kogan Page, London.

Boud, D., Keogh, R. and Walker, D. (1985) *Reflection: Turning Experience into Learning*, Kogan Page, London.

Brehm, S.S., Miller, R., Perlman, D. and Campbell, S.M. (2002) *Intimate Relations*, McGraw-Hill, New York.

Bresser, F. (2006a) Best implementation of coaching in business. Part 1. *Coach the Coach*, 20, Fenman Ltd.

Bresser, F. (2006b) Best implementation of coaching in business. Part 2. *Coach the Coach*, 21, Fenman Ltd.

British Psychological Society (2009) *Code of Ethics and Conduct*, March.

British Psychological Society (2012) *Register of Coaching Psychologists*, http://www.bps.org.uk/what-we-do/developing-profession/register-coaching-psychologists/register-coaching-psychologists (accessed 2 December 2012).

Brookfield, S.D. (1998) *Developing Critical Thinking: Challenging Adult to Explore Alternative Ways of Thinking and Acting*, Jossey-Bass, San Francisco.

Bruner, J.S. (1964) The course of cognitive growth. *American Psychologist*, 19, 1–15.

Brunner, J. (1986) *Actual Mind, Possible Worlds*, Harvard University Press, Cambridge, MA.

Buckley, A. and Buckley, C. (2006). *A Guide to Coaching and Mental Health: the Recognition and Management of Psychological Issues*, Routledge, East Sussex.

Buss, D. and Barnes, M. (1986) Preferences in human mate selection. *Journal of Personality and Social Psychology*, 50, 559–570.

Buzan, T. (2000) *The Mind Map Book*, Penguin, London.

Byrne, D. and Nelson, D. (1965) Attraction and linear function of positive reinforcements. *Journal of Personality and Social Psychology*, 1, 659–663.

Cangelosi, V. and Dill, W.R. (1965) Organizational learning: observations toward a theory. *Administrative Science Quarterly*, 10 (2), 175–203.

Cannon-Bowers, J.A. and Salas, E. (1993) Reflections on shared cognition. *Journal of Organizational Behavior*, 22, 195–202.

Carroll, M. (2006) Key issues in coaching psychology supervision. *Coaching Psychologist*, 2 (1), 4–8.

Cavanagh, M. and Lane, D. (2012a) Coaching psychology coming of age: the challenges we face in the messy world of complexity. *International Coaching Psychology Review*, 7 (1), 75–89.

Cavanagh, M. and Lane, D. (2012b) Coaching psychology coming of age: a response to our discussants. *International Coaching Psychology Review*, 7(1), 127–129.

Chambless, D.L. (1988) Empirically validated treatment, in *Psychologists' Desk Reference* (eds G.P. Koocher, J.C. Norcross and S.S. Hill), Oxford University Press, New York, pp. 209–219.

Chao, G.T., Walz, P.M. and Gardner, P.D. (1992) Formal and informal mentorships. A comparison of mentoring functions and constraints with non-mentored counterparts. *Personal Psychology*, 45, 619–636.

Chaplain, R. (2003) *Teaching Without Disruption (Volume I). A Model for Managing Pupil Behaviour in the Secondary School*, Routledge Falmer, Oxford.

Chartered Institute of Personnel and Development (2012) Coaching and mentoring, http://www.cipd.co.uk/hr-topics/coaching-mentoring.aspx#Informationpage (accessed 4 August 2012).

Chattopadhyay, P., Glick, W.H., Miller, C.C. and Huber, G.P. (1999) Determininants of executive beliefs: comparing functional conditioning and social influence, *Strategic Management Journal*, 20, 763–789.

Cherniss, C. and Adler, M. (2000) *Promoting Emotional Intelligence in Organization*, American Society for Training and Development, Alexandria, VA.

Clawson, J.G. (1976) Mentoring in the information age. *Leadership and Organisation Development Journal*, 17 (3), 6–15.

Clore, G.l. and Byrne, D. (1974) A reinforcement model of attraction, in *Foundations of Interpersonal Attraction* (ed. T.L. Huson), Academic Press, New York.

Clough, P. and Strycharczyk, D. (2012) *Developing Mental Toughness: Improving Performance, Wellbeing and Positive Behaviour in Others*, Kogan Page, London.

Clutterbuck, D. (1998) *Learning Alliances: Tapping Into Talent*, Institute of Personnel Development, London.

Clutterbuck, D. (2004) *Everyone Needs a Mentor*, 4th edn, Personnel Publication Ltd, London.

Clutterbuck, D. and Megginson, D. (2005) *Creating a Coaching Culture*, CIPD, London.

Collin, A. (1979) Notes on some typologies of managerial development and the role of mentor in the process of adaptation of the individual to the organisation. *Personnel Review*, 8 (4), 10–12.

Collins, A.M. and Quillian, M.R. (1969) Retrieval time from semantic memory. *Journal of Verbal Learning and Verbal Behaviour*, 8, 240–247.

Combrink, A., Maree, J. and Mabolo, M. (2006) Breaking the silence: stories as a tool for healing in marginalized communities. Presentation at International Narrative Therapy Festive Conference, 1–3 March, Dulwich Centre, Adelaide, Australia.

Cranton, P. (1996) *Professional Development as Tranformative Learning*, Jossey-Bass, San Francisco.

Crawford, R. (1954) *Techniques of Creative Thinking*, Hawthorn Books, New York.

Csikszentmihalyi, M. (1991) *Flow – The Psychology of Optimal Experience*, Harper Perennial, New York.

Cyert, R.M. and March, J.G. (1963) *A Behavioral Theory of the Firm*, Prentice-Hall, Englewood Cliffs, NJ.

Daloz, L. (1999) *Mentor: Guiding the Journey of Adult Learners*, Jossey-Bass, San Francisco.

Davies ,R. and Sedley, L. (2009) *Agile Coaching*, Pragmatic Bookshelf, London.

de Bono, E. (1970) *Lateral Thinking, Creativity Step by Step*, Harper & Row, New York.

de Bono. E. (1985) *Six Thinking Hats*, Penguin, London.

Department of Trade and Industry (2006) Evaluation of the impact of England's Regional Development Agencies – developing a methodology and evaluation framework, http://www.dti.gov.uk/about/evaluation/eval_guide.pdf (accessed 4 August 2012).

Didion, J. (2006) *We Tell Ourselves Stories in Order to Live: Collected Nonfiction*, Everyman's Library, London.

Doran, G.T. (1981) There's a S.M.A.R.T. way to write management's goals and objectives. *Management Review*, 70 (11), 35.

Downey, M. (1999) *Effective Coaching*, Orion Business Books, London.

Drake, D.B. (2006) Narrative coaching: the foundation and framework for a story-based practice. Narrative Matters International Conference, Wolfville, Nova Scotia.

Drake, D.B. (2007) The art of thinking narratively: implications for coaching psychology and practice. *Australian Psychologist*, 42 (4), 283–294.

Drake, D.B. (2008a) Finding our way home: coaching's search for identity in a new era. *Coaching: An International Journal of Theory, Research and Practice*, 1 (1), 15–26.

Drake, D.B. (2008b) Thrice upon a time: narrative structure and psychology as a platform for coaching, in *The Philosophy and Practice of Coaching: Issues and Insights for a New Era* (eds D.B. Drake, D. Brennan and K. Gørtz), Jossey-Bass, San Francisco, pp. 51–71.

Drake, D.B. (2009). Narrative coaching, in *The Sage Handbook of Coaching* (eds E. Cox, T. Bachkirova and D. Clutterbuck), Sage, London, pp. 120–131.

Drake, D.B. (2012) Anxiety and complexity in a postprofessional era: The challenge of practising what we preach. *International Coaching Psychology Review*, 7 (1), 106–108.

Driscoll, M.P. (2005) *Psychology of Learning for Instruction*, Pearson Education, New York.

Duffy, M. and Passmore, J. (2010) Ethics in coaching: an ethical decision making framework for coaching psychologists. *International Coaching Psychology Review*, 5 (2), 140–151.

Duncan, R. and Weiss, A. (1979) Organizational learning: implications for organizational design, in *Research in Organizational Behavior* (ed. B. Staw), JAI Press, Greenwich, CT.

Dyer, J.G. and McGuinness, T.M. (1996) Resilience: analysis of the concept. *Archives of Psychiatric Nursing*, 10 (5), 276-82.

East Mentoring Forum (2005) Embracing diversity – cross-cultural coaching and mentoring. *MentforReview*, EMF Spring.

Ebbinghaus, H. (1885, trans 1913) *Memory: A Contribution to Experimental Psychology*, Columbia University, Teacher's College Press, New York.

Ekblom, P., Law, H.C. and Sutton, M. (1996) Domestic burglary schemes in the Safer Cities Programme. Home Office RSD Research Findings No. 42, Home Office, London.

Elsbree, L. (1982) *The Rituals of Life: Pattern in Narrative*, Kennikat, New York.

EMCC (2011) Code of Conduct – for Coaching and Mentoring, http://www.emccouncil.org/src/ultimo/models/Download/102.pdf (accessed 4 August 2012).

Eyerman, R. and Jamison, A. (1991) *Social Movements: A Cognitive Approach*, Pennsylvania State University Press, University Park, PA.

Festinger, V., Schachter, S. and Back, K.W. (1950) *Social Pressures in Informal Groups: A Study of Human Factors in Housing*, Harper, New York.

Fiol, C.M. and Lyles, M.A. (1985) Organizational learning. *Academy of Management Review*, 10, 803–813.

Fischer, H. (1992) Theory of social comparison processes. *Human Relations*, 2, 117–140.

Fitzsimmons, G. and Guise, S. (2010) Coaching for leadership style, in *Leadership Coaching* (ed. J. Passmore), Kogan Page, London.

Fredrickson, B.L., Mancuso, R.A., Branigan, C. and Tugade, M.M. (2000) The undoing effect of positive emotions. *Motivation and Emotion*, 24, 237–258.

Freire, P. (1992) *Politics of Education*, Brunner/Mazel, Greenwich, CT.

Gale, J.E. (1992) *Conversation Analysis of Therapeutic Discourse: The Pursuit of a Therapeutic Agenda. Advances in Discourse Processes XLI*, Ablex, Norwood, NJ.

Gale, J.E. and Newfield, N. (1992) A conversation analysis of a solution-focused marital therapy session. *Journal of Marital and Family Therapy*, 18, 163–165.

Gallwey, T. (2000) *The Inner Game of Work*, Random House, Texene.

Gardner, H. (1983) *Frames of Mind: The Theory of Multiple Intelligences*, Basic Books, New York.

Garvey, B. (2011) *A Very Short, Fairly Interesting and Reasonably Cheap Book about Coaching and Mentoring*, Sage, London.

Garvey, R. and Garrett, H.R. (2005) The benefits of mentoring-literature review. Paper for East Mentoring Forum, February, Essex, UK.

Garvin, D.A. (1993) Building a learning organization. *Harvard Business Review*, 71 (4), 78–84.

Geertz, C. (1973) *The Interpretation of Cultures: Selected Essays*, Basic Books, New York.

Geertz, C. (1986) Anti-anti-relativism. *American Anthropologist*, 86, 263–278.

Gibb, G. (1988) *Learning by Doing: A Guide to Teaching and Learning Methods*, Oxford Brookes University, Oxford.

Gilbourne, D. (2006) Reflecting on the reflections of others: support and critique. *Sport and Exercise Psychology Review*, 2 (2), 49–54.

Gillie, M. (2009) *I and Thou*, Scribner's Sons, New York.

Ginsberg, A. (1990) Constructing the business portfolio: a cognitive model of diversification. *Journal of Management Studies*, 26, 417–438.

Goleman, D. (1995) *Emotional Intelligence, Why It Can Matter More Than IQ*, Bloomsbury, London.

Goleman, D. (1998) *Working with Emotional Intelligence*, Bloomsbury, London.

Gollwitzer, P.M., Heckhausen, H. and Ratajczak, H. (1990) Deliberative and implemental mind-sets: cognitive tuning toward congruous thoughts and information. *Journal of Personality and Social Psychology*, 59, 1119–1127.

Grant, A. and Palmer, S. (2002) Coaching Psychology Workshop. Torquay, 18 May, Annual Conference of the Division of Counselling Psychology, British Psychological Society.

Greenberger, D. and Padesky, C.A. (1995) *Mind Over Mood – Change How You Feel by Changing the Way You Think*, Guilford Press, New York.

Greene, J. and Grant, A.M. (2003) *Solution-Focused Coaching: Managing People in a Complex World*, Pearson Education, Harlow.

Grenville-Cleave, B. and Passmore, J. (2009) *The Facebook Manager: The Psychology and Practice of Web-based Social Networking*, Management Books, London.

Grimley, B. (2012) *Theory and Practice of NLP Coaching: A Psychological Approach*, Sage, London.

Grotowski, J. (1970) *Towards a Poor Theatre*, Touchstone, California.

Haberman, J. (1971) *Knowledge and Human Interest*, Heinemann, London.

Hall, L. (ed.) (2006) News: Sort it with a story from Down Under. *Coaching at Work*, 1 (2), 8.

Hamel, G. (1996) Strategy as revolution. *Harvard Business Review*, July–August, 69–82.

Handy, C.B. (1989) *The Age of Unreason*, Business Books, London.

Hart, E. and Bond, M. (1996) Making sense of action research through the use of action research. *Journal of Advanced Nursing*, 23, 1752–1759.

Hartley, J., Whomsley, S. and Clarke, I. (2006) Transpersonal encounter: honouring people's stories as a route to recovery. *The Transpersonal Psychology Review*, 10 (1), 93–101.

Hawkins, P. and Smith, N. (2006) *Coaching, Mentoring and Organizational Consultancy: Supervision and Development*, McGraw-Hill, Maidenhead.

Hefferon, K. and Boniwell, I. (2011) *Positive Psychology: Theory, Research and Applications*, McGraw-Hill, London.

Heidegger, M. (1962) *Being and Time* (trans. J. Macquarrie and E. Robinson), Basil Blackwell, Oxford.

Hergenhan, B.R.H. and Olson, M.H. (1997) *An Introduction to Theories of Learning*, Pearson, London.

Herlocker, J.L. (2000) Explaining collaborative filtering recommendations. Proceedings of CSCW, pp. 241–250.

Heron, J. (1981a) Experiential research methodology, in *Human Enquiry: A Sourcebook of New Paradigm Research* (eds P. Reason and J. Rowan), John Wiley & Sons, Ltd, Chichester.

Heron, J. (1981b) Philosophical basis for a new paradigm, in *Human Enquiry: A Sourcebook of New Paradigm Research* (eds P. Reason and J. Rowan), John Wiley & Sons, Ltd, Chichester.

Higgins, J. (ed.) (2005) Oil change. *Director*, December, 46–49.

Hill, D. and Jones, C. (eds) (2003) *Forms of Ethical Thinking in Therapeutic Practice*, Buckingham, Open University Press.

Hilpern, K. (2006) Driving force. *Coaching at Work*, 1 (2), 30–31.

HMSO (1997) *Green Book – Appraisal and Evaluation in Central Government*, The Stationery Office, London.

Hodgkinson, G.P. and Sparrow, P.R. (2002) *The Competent Organisation*, Open University Press, Buckingham.

Honey, P. and Mumford, A. (2006) *The Learning Styles Helper's Guide*, Peter Honey Ltd, Maidenhead.

Hounsell, D. (1984) Understanding teaching and teaching understanding, in *The Experience of Learning* (eds F. Marton, D. Hounsell and N. Entwistle), Scottish Academic Press, Edinburgh.

Houston, J. (1998) *A Passion for the Possible*. Thorsons, London.

Huber, G.P. (1991) Organizational learning: the contributing process and the literatures. *Organization Science*, 2 (1), 88–115.

Humphrey, S. and Holland, S. (2006) A chemistry lesson. *Coaching at Work*, 1 (2), 22–25.

Hunt, K.R. (2004) DEFRA Rural and FBAS E-Mentoring Project final evaluation. EMCC Conference Proceedings, November.

Hussain, Z., Ireland, S. and Law, H.C. (2005) Evaluation of a Universal Integrated Framework for Mentor/Coaching. European Mentoring and Coaching Council Conference Proceedings, Zurich, December.

ICF and PricewaterhouseCoopers (2012) ICF Global Coaching Study – Executive summary, http://www.coachfederation.org/coachingstudy2012 (accessed 10 June 2012).

Ireland, S., Hussain, Z. and Law, H.C. (2006) The perfect matchmaker. *Coaching at Work*, 1 (2), 26–29.

Jahoda, M. (1958) *Current Concepts of Positive Mental Health*, Basic Books, New York.

James, W. (first published 1902, 1960) *The Variety of Religious Experience: A Study of Human Nature*, Fontana, London.

Jarvis, P. (1987) Meaningful and meaningless experience: towards an analysis of learning from life. *Adult Education Quarterly*, 37 (3), 164–172.

Jarvis, P. (1992) *Paradox of Learning: On Becoming an Individual in Society*, Jossey-Bass, San Francisco.

Johnson, G. and Scholes, K. (1999) *Exploring Corporate Strategy: Text and Cases*, 5th edn, Prentice-Hall, London.

Jones, J. and Pfeiffeer, J.W. (eds) (1973) The Johari Window: a model for soliciting and giving feedback. *The 1973 Annual Handbook for Facilitators*, Pfeiffeer, San Diego.

Jung, C. (1933) *Modern Man in Search of a Soul*, Harcourt, Brace & World, New York.

Kauffman, C. and Scouler, A. (2004) Towards a positive psychology of executive coaching, in *Positive Psychology in Practice* (eds P.A. Linley and S. Joseph), John Wiley & Sons, Inc, New Jersey:

Kegan, R. (1982) *The Evolving Self: Problem and Process in Human Development*, Harvard University Press, Cambridge, MA.

Kegan, R. (1994) *In Over Our Head: The Mental Demands of Modern Life*, Harvard University Press, Cambridge, MA.

Keller, J.M. (1984). Use of the ARCS model of motivation in teacher training, in *Aspects Of Educational Technology XVII. Staff Development and Career Updating* (ed. K.E. Shaw), Nichols, New York.

Kessels, J.W.M. (1996) Knowledge productivity and the corporate curriculum, in Knowledge Management: Organization, Competence and methodology; Proceedings of 4th International ISMICK Symposium, 21–22 October, Rotterdam.

Kiesler, S., Siegel, J. and McGuire, T.W. (1984) Social psychological aspects of computer-mediated communication. *American Psychologist*, 39, 1123–1134.

Kirkpatrick, D. (1959) Evaluating training programs. *Coaching at Work*, 1 (2).

Klohnen, E.C. and Mendelsohn, G.A. (1998) Partner selection for personality characteristics. A couple centred approach. *Personality and Social Psychology Bulletin*, 24 (3), 268–278.

Kobasa, S.C. (1979) Stressful life events, personality, and health – Inquiry into hardiness. *Journal of Personality and Social Psychology*, 37 (1), 1–11.

Koffka, K. (1935) *The Principles of Gestalt Psychology*, Brace and World, Princeton, NJ.

Kogan, M. (1998) The politics of making meaning: discourse analysis of a 'post-modern' interview. *Journal of Marital and Family Therapy*, 20, 229–251.

Kogan, S.M. and Gale, J.E. (1997) Decentering therapy: textual analysis of a narrative therapy session. *Family Process*, 36, 101–126.

Kohlberg, L. (1981) *The Philosophy of Modern Development. Moral Stage and the Idea of Justice*, Harper & Row, New York.

Kolb, D.A. (1984) *Experiential Learning: Experience as the Source of Learning and Development*, Prentice Hall, Englewood Cliffs, NJ.

Koskela, L. (1992) Application of the new production philosophy in construction. Technical Report No. 72, The Center for Integrated Facility Engineering (CFIFE), Stanford University.

Kram, K.E. and Hall, D.T. (1996) Mentoring in the context of diversity and turbulence, in *Managing Human Resource Strategies for Transforming the Workplace* (eds E.E. Kossek and S. A. Lobel), Blackwell Business, Cambridge, MA, pp. 108–136.

Krause, I.-B. (1998) *Therapy Across Culture*, Sage, London.

Lane, D. (2005) Building a model for coaching psychology practice. Workshop at the second National Conference of the Special Group in Coaching Psychology in the UK. The British Psychological Society.

Lave, J. and Wenger, E. (1991) *Situated Learning – Legitimate Peripheral Participation*, Cambridge University Press, Cambridge.

Law, H.C. (2002) Coaching Psychology Interest Group – an introduction. *The Occupational Psychologist*, 47, 31–32.

Law, H.C. (2003) Applying psychology in executive coaching programmes for organisations. *The Occupational Psychologist*, 49, 12–19.

Law, H.C. (2005a) Embracing diversity – cross-cultural coaching and mentoring. *MentforReview*, Spring.

Law, H.C. (2005b) The role of ethical principles in coaching psychology. *Coaching Psychologist*, 1 (1), 19–20.

Law, H.C. (2005c) The new code of ethics, human rights, and coaching psychology. *Coaching Psychologist*, 1, (2), 13–15.

Law, H.C. (2006a) Ethical principles in coaching psychology. *Coaching Psychologist*, 2 (1), 13–16.

Law, H.C. (2006b) Can coaches be good in any context? *Coaching at Work*, 1 (2), 14.

Law, H.C. (2007) Reflection on spiritual performance in celebrating our story of 100 years of transpersonal psychology at the 10th Annual Conference. *Transpersonal Psychology Review*, 11 (1).

Law, H.C. (2010) Coaching relationships and ethical practice, in The Coaching Relationship (eds S. Palmer and A. McDowall), Routledge, London.

Law, H.C. (2012). The application of mindfulness. *Counselling Psychology Quarterly*, 26, 1–8.

Law, H.C. (2014) *The Psychology of Coaching, Mentoring and Learning*, 2nd edn, John Wiley & Sons, Ltd, Chichester.

Law, H.C. and Ackland, C. (2011) Deconstruction of the NLP Meta Model within the context of coaching at work. Paper presented at the 3rd European Conference Of Coaching Psychology hosted by BPS Special Group In Coaching Psychology, 13 and 14 December 2011. *Conference Abstracts*, City University, London.

Law, H.C., Aga, S. and Hill, J. (2006) 'Creating a "camp fire" at home', Narrative coaching–Community Coaching and Mentoring Network Conference Report and Reflection, in *The Cutting Edge* (ed. H.C. Law), Peterborough School of Arts Publication, England, Vol. 7, No. 1.

Law, H.C. and Aquilina, R. (2013) Developing a healthcare leadership coaching model using action research and systems approaches – a case study: implementing an executive coaching program to support nurse managers in achieving organizational objectives in Malta. *International Coaching Psychology Review*, 8 (1), 54–71.

Law, H.C. and FitzGerald, R. (2012). Coaching psychology in education – evaluation of coach training in Bahrain. The BPS SGCP Annual Conference, 7 December. *Conference Abstracts*, Aston University, Birmingham, UK.

Law, H.C. and Grimley, B. (2011) A Guide to NLP Coaching Psychology – Understanding and Applying NLP and Psychological Principles in Coaching. Unpublished Manuscript. Available from the author.

Law, H.C., Ireland, S. and Hussain, Z. (2005) Evaluation of Coaching Competence Self Review online tool within an NHS leadership development programme. Special Group in Coaching Psychology Annual National Conference, December, The British Psychological Society, London, City University.

Law, H.C., Ireland, S. and Hussain, Z. (2007) *The Psychology of Coaching, Mentoring and Learning*, John Wiley & Sons, Ltd, Chichester.

Law, H.C., Lancaster, L. and DiGiovanni, N. (2010) A wider role for coaching psychology – applying transpersonal coaching psychology. *The Coaching Psychologist*, 6 (1), 22–31.

Law, H.C. and Stelter, R. (2010) Multi story – coaching narrative. *Coaching at Work*, 5 (2), 28–33.

Law, H.C. and Wells, C. (2003) Championing equality – an organizational perspective and the role of psychologists. Proceedings of the Division of Occupational Psychology Annual Conference, British Psychological Society.

Lee, G. (2003) *Leadership Coaching: From Personal Insight to Organisational Performance*, CIPD, London.

Leonard, N.H., Scholl, R.W. and Kowalski, B. (1999) Information processing style and decision making. *Journal of Organizational Behavior*, 20, 407–420.

Lerner, B.S. and Locke, E.A. (1995). The effects of goal setting, self. efficiency, competition and personal traits on the performance of an endurance task. *Journal of Sport and Exercise Psychology*, 17, 138–152.

Levinson, D.J. (1997) *The Season of a Woman's Life*, Ballantine, New York.

Levinson, D.J., Darrow, D.N., Klein, E.B., Levinson, M.H. and McKee, B. (1978) *The Season of a Man's Life*, Knopf, New York.

Levitt, B. and March, J.G. (1988) Organisational learning. *Annual Review of Sociology*, 14, 319–340.

Lewin, K. (1951) Field theory in social science, in *Selected Theoretical Papers* (ed. D. Cartwright), Harper & Row, New York.

Lincoln, Y.S. and Guba, E.G. (1984) *Naturalistic Enquiry*, Sage, Newbury Park, CA.

Linley, P.A. and Harrington, S. (2005). Positive psychology and coaching psychology: perspectives on integration. *The Coaching Psychologist*, 1 (July), 13–14.

Linley, P.A. and Joseph, S. (2004) Applied positive psychology: a new perspective for professional practice, in *Positive Psychology in Practice* (eds P.A. Linley and S. Joseph), John Wiley & Sons, Inc, New Jersey.

Linley, P.A. and Joseph, S. (eds) (2004a) *Positive Psychology in Practice*, John Wiley & Sons, Inc, New Jersey.

Lioukas, S. and Chambers, D. (1998) Strategic decision-making process: the role of management and context. *Strategic Management Journal*, 19, 39–58.

Lipman-Blumen, J. (1996) *Connective Leadership: Managing in a Changing World*, Oxford University Press, New York.

Locke, E.A. and Latham, G.P. (1990) *A Theory of Goal Setting and Task Performance*, Prentice Hall, London.

Locke, E.A., Shaw, K.N., Saari, L.M. and Latham, G.P. (1981). Goal setting and task performance: 1969–1980. *Psychological Bulletin*, 90, 125–152.

Loevinger, J. and Blasi, A. (1976) *Ego Development*, Jossey-Bass, San Francisco.

Ludford, P.J. Cosley, D., Frankowski, D. and Terveen, L. (2004) Think different: increasing on-line community participation using uniqueness and group dissimilarity, in Proceedings of the SIGCHI conference on Human factors in Computing Systems, New York.

Luft, J. (1970) *Group Processes: An Introduction to Group Dynamics*, 2nd edn. National Press Books, Palo Alto, CA.

Magee, W. (2006) Two heads, one mind. *Director for Business Leaders*, November, 68–71.

Magerman, M.H. and Leahy, M.J. (2009) The lone ranger is dying: gestalt coaching as support and challenge. *International Gestalt Journal*, 32 (1), 173–196.

Marienau, C. (1999) Self-assessment at work: outcome of adult reflections on practice. *Adult Education Quarterly*, 49 (3), 135–146.

Markoczy, L. (1997) Measuring beliefs: accept no substitutes. *Academy of Management Journal*, 40, 1228–1242.

Maslow, A.H. (1954) *Motivation and Personality*, Harper & Row, New York.

Maslow, A.H. (1968) *Toward a Psychology of Being*, 2nd edn, Van Nostrand Reinhold, New York.

Mayer, J.D. and Salovey, P. (1997) What is emotional intelligence? In *Emotional Development and Emotional Intelligence: Emotional Implications* (eds P. Salovey and D.J. Sluytrer), Basic Books, New York.

Mbiti, J. (1969) *African Religions and Philosophy*, Tavistock, London.

McFee, G. (1993) Reflections on the nature of action research. *Cambridge Journal of Education*, 23, 173–183.

McGoven, J. (2001) Maximising the impact of executive coaching. *Manchester Review*, Manchester Consulting, Manchester.

McKenna, D. and Davis, S. (2009) Hidden in plain sight. *Industrial and Organizational Psychology: An Exchange of Perspectives on Science and Practice*, 3 (2), 244–260.

McKenna, K.Y.A., Green, A.S. and Gleeson, M.E. (2002) Relationship formation on the Internet: What's the big attraction? *Journal of Social Issues*, 58, 9–31.

Megginson, D. and Clutterbuck, D. (1995) *Techniques for Coaching and Mentoring*, Elsevier Butterworth-Heinemann, Oxford.

Megginson, D. and Clutterbuck, D. (2009) *Further Techniques in Coaching and Mentoring*, Butterworth Heinemann, Oxford.

Megginson, D., Stokes, P. and Garrett-Harris, R. (2003) Passport to export mentoring pilot scheme – East Midlands. An Evaluation Report on behalf of Trade Partners UK, MRCU Sheffield Hallam University, Sheffield.

Melnick, J. and Nevis, S. (2005) Gestalt methodology, in *Gestalt Therapy: History, Theory and Practice*, (eds A. Woldt and S. Toman), Sage, Thousand Oaks, CA, pp. 101–114.

Mentkowski, M. *et al.* (2000) *Learning that Lasts: Integrating Learning, Development and Performance in College and Beyond*, Jossey-Bass, San Francisco.

Merriam, S. (1994) Learning and life experience: the connection in adulthood, in *Interdisciplinary Handbook of Adult Learning* (ed. J. Sinnott), Greenwood Press, Westport, CT.

Merton, R.K. (1948) The self-fulfilling prophesy, *Antioch Review*, 8, 193–210.

Mezirow, J. (1990) *Fostering Critical Reflection in Adulthood: A Guide to Transformative and Emancipatory Learning*, Jossey-Bass, San Francisco.

Mezirow, J. (1991) *Transformative Dimensions of Adult Learning*, Jossey-Bass, San Francisco.

Mezirow, J. (1996) Contemporary paradigms of learning. *Adult Education Quarterly*, 44 (3), 158–173.

Mezirow, J. (2000) *Learning as Transformation: Critical Perspectives on a Theory in Progress*, Jossey-Bass, San Francisco.

Miller, C.C., Burke, L.M. and Glick, W.H. (1998) Cognitive diversity among upper-echelon executives: implications for strategic decision process. *Strategic management Journal*, 19, 39–58.

Mintzberg, H. (1994) The fall and rise of strategic planning. *Harvard Business Review*, January–February, 107–114.

Mischel, W. (1968) *Personality and Assessment*, John Wiley & Sons, Inc., New York.

Mohammed, S., Klimoski, R. and Rentsch, J. (2000) The measurement of team mental models: we have no shared schema. *Organizational Research Methods*, 3, 123–165.

Moon, J.A. (1999) *Reflection in Learning and Professional Development – Theory and Practice*, RoutledgeFalmer, Oxford.

Moreland, R.L. (2000) Transactive memory: learning who knows what in work groups and organizations, in *Shared Cognition in Organizations: The Management of Knowledge*. (eds L. Thompson, D. Messick and J. Levine), Erlbaum, Hillsdale, NJ.

Murray, A. (1989) Top management group heterogeneity and firm performance. *Strategic Management Journal*, 10, 125–141.

Myerhoff, B. (1980) *Number Our Days*, Simon and Schuster, New York.

Myerhoff, B. (1982) Life history among the elderly: performance, visibility and re-membering, in *A Crack in the Mirror: Reflexive Perspectives in Anthropology* (ed. J. Ruby), University of Pennsylvania Press, Philadelphia.

Myerhoff, B. (1986) Life not death in Venice: its second life, in *The Anthology of Experience* (eds V. Turner and E. Brunner), University of Illinois Press, Chicago.

Myers, I.B. (1962) *The Myers Briggs Type Indicator*, Consulting Psychologists Press, Palo Alto, CA.

Nandram, S.S. (2003) Mentoring in the flexible learning toolboxes intiative with Ron Oliver, Australian Flexible Learning Framework, Australian National Training Authority.

Naranjo, C. (1993) *Gestalt Therapy – The Attitude and Practice of an Atheoretical Experientialism.* Crown House, Carmarthen.

Neenan, M. and Palmer, S. (2001) Cognitive behavioural coaching. *Stress News*, 13 (3), 15–18.

Nonaka, I. (1991) The knowledge-creating company. *Harvard Business Review*, November–December, 96–104.

Nonaka, I. and Takeuchi, H. and Umemoto, K. (1996) A theory of organizational knowledge creation. *International Journal of Technology Management*, 11 (7/8), 833–845.

Norman, D.A. (1983) Some observations on mental models, in *Mental Models* (eds D. Gentner and A.L. Stevens), Erlbaum, Hillsdale, NJ.

O'Connor, J. and Lages, A. (2004) *Coaching with NLP: How to be a Master Coach*, Harper Element, New York.

Osborn, A. (1948) *Your Creative Power*, C. Scribner & Sons, New York.

Palmer, S. (2006) Coaching and coaching psychology: the coming of age? *Professorial Lectures*, 29 March, Middlesex University, London.

Palmer, S. (2007) Foreword, in *Psychology of Coaching, Mentoring and Learning* (eds H.C. Law, S. Ireland and Z. Hussain), Chichester: John Wiley & Sons, Ltd, p. xi.

Palmer, S. and Whybrow, A. (2004) Coaching psychology survey: taking stock. Paper at the BPS SGCP Inaugural Conference, 15 December, City University, London.

Palmer, S. and Whybrow, A. (2005) The proposal to establish a Special Group in Coaching Psychology. *Coaching Psychologist*, 1, 5–12.

Palmer, S. and Whybrow, A. (2006) The coaching psychology movement and its development within the British Psychological Society. *International Coaching Psychology Review*, 1 (1).

Palmer, S. and Whybrow, A. (2007) *The Handbook of Coaching Psychology*, Routledge, Hove, Sussex.

Palmer, S., Cooper, C. and Thomas, K. (2003) *Creating a Balance: Managing Stress.* British Library, London.

Parks, M.R. and Floyd, K. (1996) Making friends in cyberspace. *Journal of Communication*, 46, 80–96.

Parsloe, E. (1992) *Coaching, Mentoring and Assessing: A Practical Guide to Developing Competence*, Kogan Page, New York.

Pask, R. and Joy, B. (2007) *Mentoring – Coaching: A Handbook for Education Professionals*, Open University Press, Milton Keynes

Passmore, J. (ed.) (2009) *Diversity-in-Coaching*, Association for Coaching and Kogan Page, London.
Passmore, J., McMahon, G., Brennan, D., Lee, B. Christain, B. and Tenzyk, M. (2011) Using case studies for reflective practice, in *Supervision in Coaching* (ed. J. Passmore), Kogan Page, London.
Pavlov, I.P. (1927) *Conditioned Reflexes*, Oxford University Press, Oxford.
Pedlar, M.M., Burgoyne, J. and Boydel, T. (1991) *The Learning Company – A Strategy for Sustainable Development*, McGraw-Hill, London.
Peltier, B. (2001) *The Psychology of Executive Coaching – Theory and Application.* Brunner-Routledge, Taylor & Francis, Hove.
Perls, F.S. (1969) *Gestalt Therapy Verbatim*, Real People Press, Utah.
Perls, F.S. (1973) *The Gestalt Approach and Eye Witness to Therapy*, Science and Behaviour Books, Palo Alto, CA.
Perry, W.G. (1970) Cognitive and ethical growth: the making of meaning, in *The Modern American College* (eds A.W. Chickering *et al.*), Jossey-Bass, San Francisco, pp. 76–116.
Peterson, C. and Seligman, M.E.P. (2004) *Character Strengths and Virtues – A Handbook and Classification*, American Psychological Association, Oxford University Press, New York.
Peterson D.B. (2009) Book review: handbook of coaching psychology. *Coaching: An International Journal of Theory, Research and Practice*, 2 (1), 89–89.
Petrides, K.V. and Furnham, A. (2001) Trait emotional intelligence: psychometric investigation with reference to established trait taxonomies. *European Journal of Personality*, 15, 425–448.
Petrides, K.V., Frederickson, N. and Furnham, A. (2004) The role of trait emotional intelligence in academic performance and deviant behaviour at school. *Personality and Individual Differences*, 36, 277–293.
Petrides, K.V., Furnham, A. and Frederickson, N. (2004) Emotional intelligence. *The Psychologist*, 17 (10) 574–577.
Piaget, J. (1954) *The Construction of Reality in the Child*, Basic Books, New York.
Porter, M. (1996) What is strategy? *Harvard Business Review*, November–December, 61–78.
Reason, P. (ed.) (1988) *Human Enquiry in Action*, Sage, Newbury Park, CA.
Reason, P. and Rowan, J. (eds) (1981) *Human Enquiry: A Sourcebook of New Paradigm Research*, John Wiley & Sons, Ltd, Chichester.
Reiff, H.B., Hatzes, N.M. and Bramel, M.H. (2001) The relation of LD and gender with emotional intelligence in college students. *Journal of Learning Disabilities*, 34, 66–78.
Reigeluth, C.M. (1979), In search of a better way to organize instruction: the elaboration theory. *Journal of Instructional Development*, 2, 8–15.
Reigeluth, C.M. (1999a). *Instructional-design theories and models*, Vol. II, Erlbaum, Mahwah, NJ.
Reigeluth, C.M. (1999b). What is instructional-design theory and how is it changing? In *Instructional-design theories and models* (ed. C.M. Reigeluth), Erlbaum, Mahwah, NJ, pp. 5–29.

Rentsch, J.R. and Hall, R.J. (1994) Members of great teams think alike: a model of team effectiveness and schema similarity among team members. *Advances in Interdisciplinary Studies of Work Teams*, 1, 223–261.

Richards, J.T. (1999) Mutimodal therapy: a useful model for the executive coach. *Consulting Psychology Journal*, 51 (1), 24–30.

Roberts, J. (1994) Theories of adult development: research status and counselling implications, in *Handbook of Counselling Psychology* (eds S. D. Brown and R. W. Lent), John Wiley & Sons, Inc., New York.

Roger, C.R. (1963). Towards a science of the person. *Journal of Humanistic Psychology*, 3, Fall. Reproduced in Behaviorism and Phenomenology: Contasting Bases for Modern Psychology. Ed. T.W. Wann. Chicago, IL: University of Chicago Press, 1964

Rosenbaum, M.E. (1986) The repulsion hypothesis on the non-development of relationships. *Journal of Personality and Social Psychology*, 50, 729–736.

Rosinski, P. (2003) *Coaching Across Cultures*, Nicholas Brealey, London.

Rothbaum, B.O., Mesdows, E.A., Resick, P. and Foy, D.W. (2000) Cognitive behaviour therapy. *Journal of Traumatic Stress*, 13, 558–563.

Rotter, J.B. (1956) *Social Learning and Clinical Psychology*, Prentice-Hall, Englewood, Cliffs NJ.

Rowson, R. (2001) Ethical principles, in *Values and Ethics in the Practice of Psychotherapy and Counselling* (eds F.P. Barnes and L. Mudin), Open University Press, Buckingham.

Rumelhart, D.E. (1980) Schemata: the building blocks of cognition, in *Theoretical Issues in Reading Comprehension* (eds R.J. Spiro, B.C Bruce and W.F. Brewer), Erlbaum, Hillsdale, NJ.

Rumelhart, D.E. and Norman, D.A. (1978) Accretion, tuning, and restructuring: three modes of learning, in *Semantic factors in Cognition* (eds J.W. Cotton and R.L. Klatzky), Erlbaum, Hillsdale, NJ.

Rumelhart, D.E. and Norman, D.A. (1981) Analogical processes in learning, in *Cognitive Skills and their Acquisition* (ed. J.R. Anderson), Erlbaum, Hillsdale, NJ.

Rushall, B.S. (2003) Coaching development and the second law of thermodynamics [or belief-based versus evidence-based coaching development], http://www-rohan.sdsu.edu/dept/coachsci/csa/thermo/thermo.htm (accessed 8 November 2006).

Sackmann, S.A. (1991) *Cultural Knowledge in Organizations: Exploring the Collective Mind*, Sage, Newbury Park, CA.

Sackmann, S.A. (1992) Culture and sub-cultures: an analysis of organizational knowledge. *Administrative Science Quarterly*, 37, 140–161.

Safran, J.D. (1990) Towards a refinement of cognitive therapy in light of interpersonal theory. *Clinical Psychological Review*, 10, 87–105.

Salovey, P. and Mayer, J.D. (1990) Emotional intelligence. *Imagination, Cognition and Personality*, 9, 185–211.

Sartre, J.-P. (1956) *Being and Nothingness: A Phenomenological Essay on Ontology*, Taylor & Francis, London.

Schön, D.A. (1983). *The Reflective Practitioner*, Basic Books, New York.

Schön, D.A. (1991) *The Reflective Practitioner: How Professionals Think in Action*, Ashgate, London.

Schunk, D.H. and Zimmerman, B.J. (1994). Self-regulation in education: retrospect and prospect, in *Self-regulation of Learning and Performance* (eds D.H. Schunk and B.J. Zimmerman), Erlbaum, Hillsdale, NJ.

Seligman, M.E.P. and Csikszentmihalyi, M. (2000) Positive psychology: an introduction. *American Psychologist*, 55, 5–14.

Senge, P.M. (1990) *The Fifth Discipline: The Art and Practice of the Learning Organisation*, Doubleday, London.

Shams, M. and Law, H.C. (2012) Peer coaching framework: an exploratory technique. *The Coaching Psychologist*, 8 (1), 46–49.

Sheehy, G. (1977) *Passages: Predictable Crises of Adult Life*, Ballantine, New York.

Sheehy, G. (1996) *New Passages*, Ballantine, New York.

Simon, S.N. (2009) Applying gestalt theory to coaching. *Gestalt Review*, 13 (3), 230–239.

Slaski, M. and Cartwright, S. (2003) Emotional intelligence training and its implications for stress, health and performance. *Stress and Health*, 19, 233–239.

Smith, J.A. and Osborn, M. (2003) Interpretative phenomenological analysis, in *Qualitative Psychology: A Practical Guide to Research Methods* (ed. J.A. Smith), Sage, London.

Smith, K.G., Olian, J.D., Smith, K.A. and Flood, P. (1999) Top management team diversity, group process and strategic consensus. *Strategic Management Journal*, 20, 445–465.

Solomon, H.M. (2000) The ethical self, in *Jungian Thought in the Modern World* (eds E. Christopher and H.M. Solomon), Free Association, London.

Spence, G.B., Cavanagh, M.J. and Grant, A.M. (2006) Duty of care in an unregulated industry: initial findings on the diversity and practices of Australian coaches. *International Coaching Psychology Review*, 1 (1).

Spinelli, E. (2006) Applying existential psychology in a coaching psychology practice: the question of conflict. Paper presented at the Coaching Psychology Special Group's 2nd National Conference, 19–20 December, British Psychological Society.

Spinelli, E. and Horner, C. (2007) An existential approach to coaching, in *Handbook of Coaching Psychology* (eds S. Palmer and A. Whybrown), Routledge, London, pp. 118–132.

Spreitzer, G.M. (1995) Psychological empowerment in the workplace: construct definition, measurement and validation. *Academy of Management Journal*, 38 (5), 1442–1465.

Stacey, R.D. (1995) The science of complexity: an alternative perspective for strategic change processes. *Strategic Management Journal*, 16, 477–495.

Stacey, R.D. (1996) *Strategic Management and Organisational Dynamics: The Challenge of Complexity*, 2nd edn, Financial Times, London.

Stacey, R.D. (2012) Comment on debate article: Coaching Psychology Coming of Age: the challenges we face in the messy world of complexity. *International Coaching Psychology Review*, 7 (1), 91–95.

Staples, D.S., Greenaway, K. and McKeen, J.D. (2001) Opportunities for research about managing the knowledge-based enterprise. *International Journal of Management Review*, 3 (1), 1–20.

Stelter, R. (2007) Coaching: a process of personal and social meaning making. *International Coaching Psychology Review*, 2 (2), 191–201.

Stelter, R. (2009) Coaching as a reflective space in a society of growing diversity – towards a narrative, postmodern paradigm. *International Coaching Psychology Review*, 4 (2), 207–217.

Stelter, R. and Law, H.C. (2009) Narrative coaching – towards personal and social meaning-making. Master class at the Second European Conference of Coaching Psychology (December), London.

Stelter, R. and Law, H.C. (2010) Coaching – narrative-collaborative practice. *International Coaching Psychology Review*, 5 (2), 152–164.

Stokes, P. (2003) Exploring the relationship between mentoring and counselling. *British Journal of Guidance and Counselling*, 31 (1), 25–38.

Strata, R. (1989) Organizational learning – the key to management innovation. *Sloan Management Review*, Spring, 63–74.

Sutcliffe, K.M. and Huber, G.P. (1998) Firm and industry as determinants of executive perspective perception. *Strategic Management Journal*, 19, 793–807.

Sutherland, V. (2003) *Nurse Leadership Development Innovations in Mentoring and Coaching*, Modernisation Agency, NHS, London.

Swann, W. B. Jr (1990) To be adored or to be known: the interplay of self-enhancement and self verification, in *Handbook of Motivation and Cognition* (eds R.M. Sorrentino and E.T. Higgins), Guilford Press, New York, Vol. 2, pp. 408–448.

Swearingham, K. and Sinha, R. (2002) Interaction design for recommender systems, in *Proceedings of DIS*. ACM Press.

Szymanska, K. (2008) The Downward Arrow Technique. *The Coaching Psychologist*, 4 (2), 85–86.

Taylor, K., Marienau, C. and Fiddler, M. (2000) *Developing Adult Learners – Strategies for Teachers and Trainers*, Jossey-Bass, San Francisco.

Thatcher, M. (2006) Are ethical codes ethical? *Counselling Psychology Review*, 21 (3), 4–11.

Thornbury, J. (2000) *Living Culture: A Values-Driven Approach to Revitalising Your Company Culture*, Random House Business Books, London.

Thorndike, E.L. (1920) Intelligence and its use. *Harper's Magazine*, 140, 227–235.

Tinning, R. (1992) Reading action research: Notes on knowledge and human interest, *Quest*, 4, 1–4.

Turner, V. (1967) *The Forest of Symbols: Aspects of Ndemby Ritual*, Cornel Paperbacks, Ithaca.

Turner, V. and Brunner, E. (eds) (1986) *The Anthology of Experience*, University of Illinois Press, Chicago.

Vaill, P. (1996) *Learning as a Way of Being: Strategies of How to Survive in Permanent White Water*, Jossey-Bass, San Francisco.

van Nieuwerburgh, C. (2012) *Coaching in Education: Getting Better Results for Students, Educators and Parents (Professional Coaching)*, Karnac Books, London.

Veitch, R. and Griffitt, W. (1976) Good news. Bad news. Affective interpersonal effects. *Journal of Applied Social Psychology*, 6, 69–75.

Verity, P. (2006) Planning for growth, in *The Growing Business Handbook* (ed. A. Jolly), Kogan Page, London.

Vosniadou, S. and Brewer, W.F. (1987) Theories of knowledge restructuring in development. *Review of Educational Research*, 57, 51–67.

Vroom, V. (1964) *Expectancy Theory – Work and Motivation*, John Wiley & Sons, Inc, New York.

Vygotsky, L.S. ([1926] 1962) *Thought and Language*, MIT Press, Cambridge, MA.

Vygotsky, L.S. ([1926] 1978) *Mind in Society*, Harvard University Press, Cambridge, MA.

Walther, J.B. (1996) Interpersonal effects of computer-mediated interaction. *A Relational Perspective Communication Research*, 19 (1), 52–90.

Ward, P. (1997) *360-Degree Feedback*, Institute of Personnel and Development, London.

Weick, K.E. (1995) *Sensemaking in Organizations*, Sage, Thousand Oaks, CA.

Weick, K.E. and Roberts, K.H. (1993) Collective mind in organization: heedful interrelating on flight decks. *Administrative Science Quarterly*, 38, 357–381.

Weissman, A. (2008) Lesson learnt from Enron: a lawyer's perspective on business ethics. Keynote address at Real World Real People, Professional Ethics Conference (1–3 July 2008), Kingston University, Surrey, UK.

Wenger, E. (1998) *Communities of Practice: Learning, Meaning and Identity*. Cambridge University Press, Cambridge.

Wenger, E. (2009) Social learning capability: four essays on innovation and learning in social systems. *Social Innovation, Sociedade e Trabalho*, Booklets 12 – separate supplement, MTSS/GEP and EQUAL Portugal, Lisbon.

Wenger, E. (2011) What is a community of practice? Posted by Team BE on 28 December, in FAQs, http://wenger-trayner.com/resources/what-is-a-community-of-practice/ (accessed 4 August 2012).

Wenger, E., McDermott, R. and Snyder, W. (2002) *Cultivating Communities of Practice – A Guide to Managing Knowledge*, Harvard Business School Press, Cambridge, MA.

Wenger, E., White, N. and Smith, J.D. (2009) *Digital Habitats; Stewarding Technology for Communities*, Cpsquare.org.

Western, S. (2012) *Coaching and Mentoring – A Critical Text*, Sage, London.

White, M. (1995a) *Re-Authoring Lives: Interviews and Essays*, Dulwich Centre Publications, Adelaide.

White, M. (1995b) Reflecting team-work as definitional ceremony, in *Re-Authoring Lives: Interviews and Essays*, Dulwich Centre Publications, Adelaide..

White, M. (1997) Definitional ceremony, in *Narratives of Therapists' Lives* (M. White), Dulwich Centre Publications, Adelaide.

White, M. (2000) Reflecting team-work as definitional ceremony revisited, in *Reflections on Narrative Practice* (M. White), Dulwich Centre Publications, Adelaide.

White, M. (2006) Narrative Therapy Intensive Workshop, 20–24 February, Dulwich Centre, Adelaide.

White, M. (2007) *Maps of Narrative Practice*, Norton, New York.

White, M. and Morgan, A. (2006) *Narrative Therapy with Children and Their Families*, Dulwich Centre Publications, Adelaide.

Whiteley, P. (2006) Pioneering medicine. *Coaching at Work*, 1 (2), 30–31.

Whitmore, J. (2002) *Coaching for Performance*, Nicholas Brealey, London.

Whybrow, A. (2008) Coaching psychology: Coming of age? *International Coaching Psychology Review*, **3** (3), 227–240.

Whybrow, A. and Palmer, S. (2006) Shifting perspectives: one year into the development of the British Psychological Society Special Group in Psychology in the UK. *International Coaching Psychology Review*, 1 (2), 75–85.

Wiersema, M.F. and Bantel, K.A. (1992) Top management team demography and corporate strategic change. *Academy of Management Journal*, 35, 91–121.

Willis, P. (2005) Standards research. Proceedings of the European Mentoring and Coaching Council Annual Conference, Zurich.

Wills, T.A. (1991) Social support and interpersonal relationships, *Review of Personality and Social Psychology*, 2, 26–89.

Wong, C.S. and Law, K.S. (2002) The effects of leader and follower emotional intelligence on performance and attitude. *Leadership Quarterly*, 13, 243–274.

Zack, M. (1999) Managing codified knowledge. *Sloan Management Review*, Summer, 37–56.

Index